MAKING SUPPER SAFE

MAKING SUPPER
SAFE

One Man's Quest to Learn the Truth
about Food Safety

BEN HEWITT

RODALE.

Rodale books may be purchased for business or promotional use or for special sales. For information, please write to:
Special Markets Department, Rodale, Inc., 733 Third Avenue, New York, NY 10017

Printed in the United States of America
Rodale Inc. makes every effort to use acid-free ♾, recycled paper ♻.

Book design by Chris Gaugler

Library of Congress Cataloging-in-Publication Data is on file with the publisher.

ISBN–13: 978–1–60529–309–7

Distributed to the trade by Macmillan
2   4   6   8   10   9   7   5   3   1   hardcover

We inspire and enable people to improve their lives and the world around them.
www.rodalebooks.com

To Penny, Fin, and Rye, who nourish me in ways food cannot

1

"What's that?"

Edward leaned forward, peering through the windshield. It was night, and a searing cold had settled over the landscape, riding on a driven wind that had swept snow across the roads, where it had turned to ice and upended numerous cars along Vermont's Interstate 89. Everything looked lunar and foreboding. Already, barely 20 minutes into our drive, we had passed a Toyota truck lying on its side, illuminated by the flashing lights of emergency rescue vehicles. A few miles later, we passed an overturned sedan, its crumpled nose pressed against the ice-rimed surface of a rock face. I thought I saw one of its wheels still spinning; the front passenger door hung open, but the interior of the car was dark and I could not see if it was still occupied.

I followed Edward's gaze. Ahead of us, illuminated by the wash of our headlights, a deer lay at the base of a guardrail. Edward turned to me, and although I did not know him well,

I knew him well enough that I didn't have to guess what he was thinking: food.

The car shimmied on the ice as we came to a stop at the highway's edge. We stepped into the glacial air, our breath pluming into the dark. A row of cars passed, tires buzzing on the icy tarmac. I bent over the deer and tucked an ungloved hand into the fold of fur where leg met body. Still warm. This was a fresh kill, a coveted prize. We grabbed its legs, Edward at the front and me at the rear, and hoisted the deer into the back of my car, where it lay atop a pair of jumper cables and a rusty tire iron. "What a blessing," Edward said as we slipped back into the car and its welcome cocoon of warmth. I slid the shifter into gear, and we pulled onto the highway.

We had our meat. It was time to find some cheese.

I suppose it's simplest to say that Edward Gunny is a dumpster diver, although it's probably not fair to define a man solely by his predilection for digging through trash in search of his supper. Still, it's worth noting that Gunny, a lean-framed 28-year-old of middling height and possessing a laconic-but-not-quite-sleepy countenance, sources at least one-third of his calories from the garbage and has been doing so for nearly a decade. Given that history, and given that I've personally observed the man waist deep in garbage in pursuit of his lunch, I don't feel too badly calling him a dumpster diver.

When I first learned of Gunny's habit, I was quick to assume it meant that he ate poorly. I imagined dented cans of soup, spore-dotted loaves of bread, and the picked-over remnants of Big Macs. But he was keen to correct me and, when I asked, eager to demonstrate his prowess. "Sure, I'll take you out," he said, and he proceeded to reel off a list of his greatest scores. Aged goat cheese and specialty chocolates. Strawberries, fresh and frozen. Wine ("and not the cheap stuff," he assured me). Boxes upon boxes of Alaskan salmon fillets, admittedly a little suspect at the edges, but nothing a sharp knife and an easy hand with the spices couldn't take care of. In the nonfood category, he was particularly proud of a recent haul of 60 insulated winter jackets with only minor blemishes (he sent the bulk of the jackets to a friend in Philadelphia, to be distributed to needy families).

Why, just 2 weeks prior to our outing, he'd snagged more than 50 pounds of imported brie from a dumpster in Burlington, Vermont. For the Christmas holiday, Edward had hauled a few pounds of the stash to his family's home in southern New Hampshire. He then proceeded to bake it in his mother's oven and serve it to the assembled guests. "Where did you get this brie? It's delicious," asked his aunt, as she slid another spoonful of gooey-warm cheese between her lips. Not wanting to diminish her obvious pleasure, and yet not able to bring himself to tell an outright lie (this is the sort of fellow he is), Edward took the middle path: "Oh, it's from a store I go to all the time."

And so we embarked on that bitter December night in search of the good stuff. It was only days past Christmas, and we considered the ways in which this might work to our advantage. "They'll probably be tossing extra holiday inventory," I offered. Edward nodded, then added: "Or maybe because they were closed for a few days, a bunch of stuff went bad." I nodded. "Or maybe," I noted sagely, "with the economy so bad, they made a lot of extra inventory and had to get rid of it." This was basically

3

a repeat of my first point, but Edward didn't seem to notice or, if he did, was too kind to mention it.

I picked him up at the house he rents for $400 with his friend David, a builder of straw-bale homes who sports a gold-capped front tooth and spends his spare hours refining his musculature with a kettlebell, a simple contraption that consists of a 35-pound steel ball with a handle. "I'll show you a few moves," he said, when Edward took a phone call. And he proceeded to crank out a dozen deep knee bends with the ball hanging from his meaty hands like a penance for some earlier transgression.

The house was decorated in a style I'll call "rural bachelor rustic," which basically means that David and Edward live as if they occupy a parallel universe, where everything is oriented around an old woodstove and things like women and toilet bowl cleaner have yet to be invented. To contain heat, the upstairs had been closed off, leaving the single, first-story room to serve as bedroom, living room, and kitchen for both Edward and David. Beds were tucked into opposite corners; Edward's was open to the room, but David had troubled himself to fashion a thin privacy curtain from what looked to be old sheets. A large woodstove was central to the space, with an aged couch pulled close. Above the stove, a rack of deer antlers was mounted on a post; wool socks with blown-out heels hung from its points. The wood floor around the stove was pockmarked with charred burns from errant embers; I looked for a fire extinguisher, did not find one, and made studious note of the nearest exit. A circular table held a can of whipped cream (dumpstered), a log of butter (dumpstered), a container of sour cream (dumpstered), and a jar of kimchi, a fermented vegetable medley of Korean origin. David had made it, and he offered me a bite. Unable to source a clean utensil, and finding the dirty ones too dirty to risk, I used the tip of my pocketknife to spear a chunk of cabbage. It was insanely good. I speared another chunk, then rinsed my knife under a kitchen sink faucet that consisted of two garden hose shutoffs. It was not hard to imagine Edward and David growing old in this space, spending their days feeding the woodstove, padding around in soiled long johns, and emitting voluminous kimchi burps.

As Edward finished his call, and immediately after I completed a wobbly set of kettlebell deep knee bends (35 pounds never felt so heavy, and I earned not only a kink in my lower back but a new respect for David), David delivered a quick primer in dumpster-diving philosophy. "There is one question the dumpster diver seeks to answer," he told me, his gold tooth gleaming in the light from a bare bulb. "And that is, 'Why was this thrown away?'"

I understood immediately that David wasn't asking the question to express his concern over the food's safety but rather to indicate his distaste for capitalism and the profligate waste it often engenders. Already, I'd come to understand that among Edward and his dumpster-diving cohorts, rage against the capitalist machine is a defining motivation. This could be seen as biting the hand that feeds, for if it weren't for free-market capitalism and the inevitable waste it generates, the quantity of well-stocked dumpsters would likely decline. "It's important to not get so attached that we perpetuate the system," explained Edward, when I pointed this out. "Being bummed out that there aren't more dumpsters isn't part of the equation." And yet, I sensed a degree of conflict between Edward's anticapitalist mores and his obvious delight at sniffing out a garbage bag full of brie. Indeed, Edward's lifestyle and identity had clearly been forged, at least in part, by his gleaning habits. It seemed to me that letting go of this, even if it meant the demise of the corporatism he railed against, might be harder than he imagined.

One might assume, as I had, that unblemished food would be the dumpster diver's holy grail. But as we embarked on our quest, weaving cautiously through snow-slick turns on the secondary roads that led to the highway, Edward expounded on the benefits of food with obvious flaws. "It's nice to know why they threw it away. If it's got mold, or the package is ripped, or it's physically deformed in some way, you know what's going on with it." Another incongruity: The more perishable a product, the more Edward trusts its integrity. "The thing about meat and dairy is it gets thrown out real quick. They don't take any chances with that stuff." To be honest, this comment threw me a bit; it was the first time I seriously considered the wisdom of Edward's food-sourcing habits. I mean, I was down with the whole anticapitalist-waste-stream-diversion gig. Totally. But eating meat someone had discarded for reasons I could only guess at? Maybe I'm showing my age here, but that sounds kind of . . . I don't know . . . risky?

Fortunately, tonight we were after cheese, a favorite of Edward's in part because the region is lousy with artisanal cheese makers and in part because it's a food essentially built on fungi. This makes it susceptible to superficial mold that ruins the cheese's salability but is basically harmless and particularly easy to remove. That, and cheese tastes good, which might sound sort of banal and obvious but is actually really, really important, because dumpster diving tends to result in large stores of a singular food. Serious divers are born with the will (or have cultivated the skill; I'm not sure which) to eat the same thing day in, day out, until they've exhausted the score and can move on to the next. It is frowned upon to throw away food you've rescued from the garbage, and divers will go to great lengths to distribute anything they can't personally consume before it goes bad. Or, perhaps more accurately, badder.

At this point, it seemed entirely reasonable to bring up the issue of illness, which I'd previously skirted mostly because I didn't want Edward to think I was a ninny. But now the guy was talking about eating meat out of the trash; he'd fed dumpstered cheese to his blood relations, and over the holidays, no less. It was definitely time to go there.

Turns out, Edward *has* gotten sick from dumpster food. Once. In 10 years of committed diving. He has not forgotten the details because the details are not forgettable. "I was out late, partying a little bit, and we were just walking around town, having fun. And I dipped into the trash, and there was a half-gallon jug of Fresh Samantha Mango Mama. It was all sealed up and everything. And suddenly, I was so, so thirsty. I hadn't known I was so thirsty. I hadn't known it was possible to be so thirsty." It sounded to me as if Edward were rather drunk, but I kept my mouth shut.

In any event, drunk or not, Edward did exactly what you'd expect a parched dumpster diver to do when finding a half-gallon jug of juice in the garbage: He cracked the cap and put back a solid, uninterrupted quart of Mango Mama. Glug, glug, glug. I'll spare you the rest of the particulars, as I wish Edward had spared me, and simply say this: It didn't stay put back for long.

The Fresh Samantha incident stuck with me throughout the night, as Edward and I traveled a circuit of his favorite trash receptacles. At Ye Olde Cheese Worx (business names have been changed to protect future accessibility), we clambered into a dumpster where, amid typical office detritus, we happened upon a few dozen pounds of artisanal Cheddar and numerous packages of sweet butter. A few doors down, at the Center for Aged Fruits and Vegetables, we didn't even have to wallow in the garbage: Next to the dumpster, so close that its side actually touched the cold, brown metal, sat a pallet of organic strawberries. Did they practically throw themselves into the back of my car? They did indeed, as did a stash of Italian vinaigrette, hundreds of servings in convenient single-serving packets. "I love condiments," Edward told me unnecessarily, after wedging four boxes of salad dressing between the deer and the dairy.

By midnight, the shocks in the back of my Subaru had become compressed and useless under the load; with every pothole, an alarming thump resonated from under the car. With the deer and the cheese and the butter and the dressing (the strawberries weighed hardly anything), our haul had to be pushing 300 pounds. The sky had cleared, and the temperature had plummeted further. It was well below zero, and I felt suddenly exhausted and vulnerable. Even with the benefit of heavily insulated work gloves, my fingers burned, except for the tip of the middle left, which had surrendered all sensation. Clearly, it was time to go home.

But first, I needed a snack. Being the snacking sort, I'd anticipated this moment and had cleverly perched a chunk of cheese atop the defroster vent so that at least its edges might soften a bit. I reached for it now and tore into the plastic wrapping with my teeth, inhaling the aroma of aged Cheddar. It smelled just fine; which is to say, it smelled funky, but no funkier than the cheese I regularly purchased for upwards of $12 per pound at the local health food store. In the glow of the dash, I searched for visible mold. I couldn't find any, but then again, my Subaru is 15 years old, and a handful of burned-out dash lights is part of the toll those years have extracted. I wondered if perhaps I should wait until I got home, where I could examine the cheese under the glare of 80 watts. But I was suddenly ravenous, amazingly, profoundly hungry. I hadn't known it was even possible to be so hungry.

"What do you think?" I asked Edward. "Is it safe?" I held the cheese in my right hand and steered the car with my left. The skeletal outlines of leafless trees rushed by my window.

Edward laughed. And frankly, I couldn't be sure if he was laughing at my question because he assumed it was sincere (it was), or because he assumed it was joke, or if he was simply finding mirth in the delightful absurdity of the whole scene: two men careening through a winter's night, their car laden with enough artisanal food to feed them for a month. We had hundreds, if not thousands, of dollars' worth of food in our possession, and it had cost us nothing more than a gallon or two of gas, a few hours of missed sleep, and the ability to feel things with the tip of one finger.

I figured that if I waited a minute, Edward would stop laughing and answer my question. But he didn't, and I was hungry.

So I shrugged my shoulders. And took a bite.

9

2

I'll dispense with any lingering suspense over my well-being (thanks for your concern) and tell you now: The cheese did not make me sick. Nor did the venison, which Edward and I butchered on his kitchen table the next day, as Parliament-Funkadelic thumped from a pair of high-end stereo speakers he'd plucked from the trash a few years prior. They buzzed only a little. The strawberries turned out to be moldy beyond salvation (hey, a guy's gotta have some standards); the salad dressing, I left to Edward. Last time I saw him, he exhibited his usual good cheer, so I'm assuming the dressing went down just fine and, perhaps more important, stayed there.

Was I a bit anxious when, a few days later, I placed a chèvre-crusted venison loin roast atop our dinner table before the expectant forks of my incredibly trusting family? Why yes, I was, although I'd already sampled each ingredient myself, emboldened by the recent acquisition of a health insurance policy with a modest deductible and the apparent good health of my dumpstering mentor. Following each sampling, I experienced a period that is most politely described as "heightened intestinal awareness," during which I felt an almost supersensory connection to my digestive tract. This was not an awareness I intend to cultivate, but I'd argue that a certain degree of anxiety over consuming garbage is entirely appropriate. Heck, it could probably be counted as an evolutionary advantage, like opposable thumbs or the urge to procreate.

But lately, anxiety over whether our food is fit to eat hasn't been confined to neophyte dumpster divers. The evidence of this is not difficult to find: It is splashed across the front pages of our newspapers, is wrapped into prime-time television specials, and in particular thrives in every nook and cranny of the Internet. Google "food safety" and you'll get 150 million hits; that's about 300 percent more than you'll get for "terrorism" (43 million), and about 1,800 percent more than you'll get if you search "Mick Jagger" (8.5 million).

This type of collective anxiety is too often based in anecdotes and assumptions, but in the case of foodborne illness, the numbers seem to justify our national unease. According to the Centers for Disease Control and Prevention (CDC), more than 200,000 Americans are sickened by food every day, and each year 325,000 of us will be hospitalized because we ate contaminated food. Most tragically, over the next 52 weeks, 5,194 of us will die from a foodborne condition. That means more Americans die every year from eating contaminated food than have been killed in Iraq since the outset of the war. The victims will be disproportionately young, because the young (and in particular, children under age 4) have immature immune systems that are poorly equipped to defend against invading bacteria.

There is no shortage of acute afflictions that can be caught by eating; the CDC counts more than 200 known afflictions that are readily transmitted via food. Having become accustomed to a steady diet of headlines recounting the dangers of illness by foodborne pathogenic bacteria, I'd long assumed that the vast majority of foodborne illness is bacterial in nature. But according to the CDC, which has built its assumptions almost entirely on a 1999 study authored by Paul Mead, a medical epidemiologist with the Foodborne and Diarrheal Diseases Branch of the CDC (wow, sounds like an uplifting job, eh?), bacterial agents account for only 30.2 percent of total foodborne illnesses, while viruses account for 67.2 percent, and parasites the remaining 2.6 percent. Still, when it comes to death by foodborne illness, bacteria reign supreme, with 71.7 percent of all mortalities by food contamination (viruses come second, with 21.2 percent, and parasites third, with 7.1 percent).

Now, it's important to note that the Mead study is not without significant faults. Indeed, the oft-repeated assertion that foodborne diseases cause 76 million illnesses, 325,000 hospitalizations, and 5,194 deaths in the United States annually is no better than an educated guess; the actual tally may be worse. Most damning is the line near the end of the study that reads: "Unknown agents account for approximately 81 percent of foodborne illnesses and hospitalizations and 64 percent of deaths." In other words, a significant majority of assumed illnesses, hospitalizations, and deaths are just that: assumed. Their numbers are merely extrapolated from estimates of all deaths by gastroenteritis of unknown cause. Indeed, the extrapolation accounts for 3,400 of the total study estimate of 5,194 deaths annually.

Confused yet? If not, wait 'til you hear this: The category of estimated deaths of gastroenteritis of unknown cause is assumed to include all deaths from unknown foodborne agents. But, of course, some foodborne agents *do not* cause gastroenteritis. And at least some deaths attributed to gastroenteritis of unknown cause were caused by known agents that simply weren't detected. Misdiagnosis, if you will.

What does this all mean regarding the widespread assumption of 76 million illnesses, 325,000 hospitalizations, and 5,194 deaths annually by foodborne agents? Are we talking even *more* suffering, or less? Actually, it's probably both, because Mead's study omits potential deaths from unknown foodborne agents that do not cause gastroenteritis, while it almost certainly overstates the number of deaths from unknown foodborne agents that *do* cause gastroenteritis. (I would be remiss not to acknowledge the work of Paul D. Frenzen, a U.S. Department of Agriculture demographer who came to these conclusions in 2004 after careful review of the Mead study.)

In any event, while we can debate endlessly how many people are actually getting sick and dying from foodborne illness, one fact is inescapable: The outbreaks are getting bigger. Reading outbreak reports spanning only a few decades is almost enough to make one nostalgic for the not-so-long-ago days when victims could be counted in the dozens or, sometimes, single numbers. In the major outbreak of 1963, two women died from botulism in canned tuna; in 1974, salmonella in unpasteurized cider sickened 200 in New Jersey. Even as

recently as 1996, the big foodborne illness news was an outbreak of *E. coli* linked to apple juice; one toddler died and
another 60 or so people were sickened.

Compare these tragic but relatively isolated outbreaks to
the 21st-century outbreaks that have dominated headlines in
recent years.

☆ 2010: Half a billion eggs recalled, with 1,800-plus people
   sickened

☆ 2009: An estimated 22,500 people sickened by salmonel-
   losis in peanut butter from a single facility

☆ 2008: A rare strain of salmonella linked to fresh salsa
   causes at least 1,442 (and as many as 40,000) illnesses
   and at least one death in 43 states

☆ 2007: Two enormous beef recalls, totaling more than 27
   million pounds

I could go on, but you get the picture. Over the past few
decades, foodborne illness has shifted from being a fairly
regionalized threat with the potential to sicken a handful of
people in a single outbreak to a national hazard capable of fell-
ing thousands, if not tens of thousands, of consumers from a
single point of contamination.

Now that I've got you good and scared, please allow me to
make you downright terrified. Concurrent with the vastly
increasing scale and scope of our nation's foodborne-illness outbreaks, we have seen the rapid emergence of a number of particularly virulent bacteria.

I'm speaking primarily of *Escherichia coli* O157:H7, *Listeria monocytogenes*, *Campylobacter jejuni*, *Cyclospora cayetanensis*, and the increasing threat from the dirty half-dozen strains of non-O157 pathogenic *E. coli*, which have begun showing up— mostly in ground beef—with increasing frequency.

It should be said that it's entirely possible that these strains have existed for years, if not centuries, and that the reason we're starting to find them isn't so much because they're new but because we've never before looked. But it is also possible that at least some of these *are* new threats, the inevitable result of bacterial evolution. Because that is what bacteria do: They change. They shift. They evolve. And, like humans, they do this primarily to increase the likelihood of their survival. All of which can only make one wonder: What's going to happen over the next 30 years?

Of course, the future has a sticky tendency to be unknowable, leaving us with the inexact sciences of extrapolation, prediction, and outright guesswork when it comes to considering how the issue of food safety will evolve. But like most views forward, the view of food safety's future can be made clearer by something we *can* know with certainty: its history.

In the case of food safety, that's a relatively recent history, because while it is safe to say that there has always been foodborne illness, it is also rather difficult to quantify. The gathering and dissemination of foodborne-illness data are relatively new phenomena, sparked in large part by an acute period of public unease following the 1906 release of Upton Sinclair's seminal book *The Jungle*, which famously depicted the deplorable conditions in Chicago's stockyards and meatpacking facilities.

As one of America's original muckrakers, Sinclair had intended his tale to serve as an ode to the plight of these laborers, who worked 12-hour days and were frequently injured in an antiquated version of what is still the most dangerous factory job in our nation. But what really caught the public's attention were the book's passages regarding tuberculosis in beef and tales of men tumbling into industrial grinders and being packaged along with four-legged flesh: *"As for the other men, who worked in tank-rooms full of steam, and in some of which there were open vats near the level of the floor, their peculiar trouble was that they fell into the vats; and when they were fished out, there was never enough of them left to be worth exhibiting—sometimes they would be overlooked for days, till all but the bones of them had gone out to the world as Durham's Pure Leaf Lard!"* The tale was fiction, but like most good fiction, it held an element of truth, and the public seemed to understand this. Still, Sinclair was famously but perhaps naively surprised by the reaction: "I aimed at the public's heart, and by accident I hit it in the stomach," he said at the time.

Accidental or not, it was an important hit, in no small part because it reached the height of the American political landscape. President Theodore Roosevelt was reportedly physically sickened after reading a copy of the book; on his recovery, he immediately called on Congress to pass the Pure Food and Drugs Act of 1906, which established the Food and Drug Administration (FDA) and instituted the United States' first federal inspection standards for meat. In truth, the FDA had already existed as a science-based entity for nearly a half century; it was known as the Division of Chemistry and, at its outset, consisted of a single chemist operating under the purview of the US Department of Agriculture.

Prior to 1906, the Division of Chemistry had no regulatory powers, but in 1882 it came to be headed by Harvey Washington Wiley, a chemist and an MD possessing an almost obsessive fascination with the health effects of common food additives. Wiley applied this fascination to research into the adulteration and misbranding of food and drugs on the American market, and in 1887, he began the publication of a 10-part series called *Foods and Food Adulterants*. This was arguably the beginning of America's public awareness of food safety. Wiley received a significant boost in 1902, when Congress appropriated $5,000 to the Division of Chemistry for research into the effects of preservatives on human volunteers. The "poison squad" studies, as they became known, drew widespread attention to the issue and to the fact that the food and drug industries operated with complete autonomy.

The passage of the Pure Food and Drugs Act was the beginning of widespread food-based regulation in America, although it's interesting to note that the focus wasn't so much on pathogenic bacteria as it was on adulterants that were added intentionally. One early upshot was a legal fracas known as *United States v. Forty Barrels and Twenty Kegs of Coca-Cola*, whereby the government attempted to outlaw the drink for its excessive caffeine content, describing it as a beverage that produced serious mental and motor deficits. The ruling went in Coca-Cola's favor, but the publicity was enough to convince the manufacturer that perhaps a little less caffeine was a good idea after all.

Still, these were the early days of food-based regulation and the study of foodborne illness, and there wasn't a huge quantity of data floating around. But it's hard to imagine that just because we didn't have the data, we didn't have bacteria and illness. After all, the refrigerator didn't come on the scene until the 1920s, and it was many years before it rose to ubiquity, in no small part because, as a nascent technology, electric refrigeration commanded quite the premium: One early commercial model, a 9-cubic-foot box that boasted a water-cooled compressor and wooden case, sold in 1922 for $714. To put that in context, consider that the very same year, a Model T Ford cost approximately $450. These days, the average price of a new car is $28,000, while a new fridge can be had for less than 500 bucks. This is bad if you want to drive somewhere, but very, very good if you like cold beer.

There's little question that life before refrigeration held certain risks pertaining to the growth and dissemination of foodborne illness, but since the numbers don't exist, we'll have to be content with merely visualizing the woes wrought by rancid meats and week-old milk. Actually, given that in 1920 only 20 percent of American homes featured a flush toilet, perhaps it's better that we don't.

Beginning in 1925, just as electric refrigerators were redefining food storage (for the affluent, at least), the US Public Health Service published summaries of outbreaks of gastrointestinal illness attributed to milk; in 1938, the PHS added summaries of outbreaks from all foods to its misery list. But the level of detail and thoroughness of reporting were skimpy, and the annual summaries were primarily reactive. The most important result of these reports was the creation of the Standard Milk Ordinance (now known as the Pasteurized Milk Ordinance, or PMO), a voluntary regulatory model for the production, processing, packaging, and sale of milk and its ancillary products. Forty-six of the US states have adopted the PMO; California, Pennsylvania, New York, and Maryland have not, although they have passed laws that are similar in their stipulations and oversight. The PMO maintains that "only Grade A pasteurized, ultra-pasteurized, or aseptically processed milk and milk products shall be sold to the final consumer, to restaurants, soda fountains, grocery stores, or similar establishments." (Soda fountains? Do those even exist anymore?)

In any event, the monitoring and dispensing of data relating to foodborne illness continued pretty much in this vein for a number of decades, though it slowly became a more collaborative venture, with states and disparate governmental agencies joining forces to deliver a more complete and nuanced accounting. But there was little sense of urgency among the citizenry; for the most part, foodborne illness still felt like something that happened to other people, and as such, there was little pressure exerted on our political leaders and thus on our nation's regulatory bodies.

Part of this was due to the relatively isolated nature of foodborne-illness outbreaks in the still-developing interstate food system; in the first half of the 20th century, food production and distribution remained relatively localized affairs. Indeed, arguably the greatest foodborne-illness scare of this era was botulism; between 1899 and 1969, there were 1,696 cases attributed to 659 botulism outbreaks, 60 percent of which were transmitted by home-canned vegetables (botulism spores can survive temperatures as high as 250°F, making them impervious to most home canning methods, which top out around 240°F). This works out to about 2.5 cases per incidence, which seems almost laughable when compared to recent outbreaks.

Which is not to say that foodborne botulism is something to be taken lightly. Left untreated, its symptoms generally progress from relative mild afflictions like double vision and drooping of eyelids (heck, this happens to me anytime I drink more than two beers at a sitting), to weakness in the limbs, then to outright respiratory failure, resulting in death. Botulism is still around, to the tune of about 150 US cases annually, but only a handful of these are food related (you can also contract botulism through an open wound or by ingesting it independent of food; this is particularly common in infants). And while the bacterium is still likely to kill you if left to its own devices, advances in treatment have dropped the mortality rate from 90 percent to about 4 percent.

In 2007, eight people contracted botulism poisoning from canned foods produced by Castleberry's Food Company. It was the first incidence of botulism poisoning in commercial canned foods in over 3 decades. All of the victims recovered.

In part because of the isolated nature of botulism outbreaks, in part because of the regional nature of the era's media coverage of all foodborne-illness outbreaks (imagine: a world before Twitter and Facebook), and in part because the outbreaks never sickened that many people concurrently, getting acutely, seriously sick from food still felt like something that happened to other people.

It's not hard to define the precise moment when the vast majority of Americans stopped viewing foodborne illness as someone else's problem: January 13, 1993. That's the day the Washington Department of Health (WDOH) was notified that an unusually high number of children had been admitted to Seattle-area hospitals with confirmed cases of hemolytic uremic syndrome (HUS). HUS is secondary to *E. coli* infection; it is often (but not always) an indicator of poisoning by a strain known as *E. coli* O157:H7. Contracting HUS is like winning the bad-luck lottery of foodborne illness; it carries the potential to completely shut down the kidneys. While 90 percent of those affected survive the condition's acute phase, many are stricken with lifelong complications that can include high blood pressure, blindness, paralysis, and end-stage renal failure. The other 10 percent—children and the elderly, mostly—do not survive the first week or two. Death by HUS is a particularly unpleasant affair, being preceded by a period of intense vomiting, bloody diarrhea, and fluid accumulation in the tissues. Because patients with HUS cannot rid themselves of excess fluid and waste, they are not allowed to drink anything, even water, and suffer terrible thirst as their organs slowly shut down. I don't know about you, but I can think of about 100 ways I'd rather die.

Apparently, the staff at WDOH felt the same and took this report very seriously, launching a full-blown epidemiologic investigation that quickly turned up one striking similarity: The patients had all visited Jack in the Box restaurants in the days prior to becoming ill. And what do people go to Jack in the Box restaurants for? I'll give you a hint: It ain't tofu smoothies and bean sprouts. No sir, they go for meat. Ground beef. Hamburger.

In fact, each of the patients suffering from HUS had ordered a hamburger during their sojourn to Jack in the Box.

Ultimately, the outbreak strain of *E. coli* O157:H7 was traced to 11 lots of hamburger patties produced on November 29 and 30, 1992, by a California beef processing outfit called Vons Companies. Jack in the Box issued a recall, but the horse (or in this case, cow) had most definitely left the stable: The beef had already been distributed to franchises in California, Idaho, Nevada, and Washington, and only 20 percent of the implicated meat was recoverable. The rest had already been sold and, presumably, consumed. By the end of February 1993, 171 people who'd eaten at the 73 affected Jack in the Box restaurants had been hospitalized. Four had died; all were children. The origin of the offending *E. coli* O157:H7 was never definitively found.

The Jack in the Box incident was a major turning point for the gathering of foodborne-illness data in the United States. Shortly thereafter, the CDC launched two programs designed to bolster its ability to track and understand outbreaks. Being an agency of government, the CDC felt compelled to saddle these new programs with odd, futuristic-sounding titles that do little to explain the agenda: FoodNet and PulseNet (note the lack of proper spacing between words and never again doubt the CDC's hipness). I won't bore you with the gritty details; suffice to say that FoodNet was designed to bolster the agency's grasp of the epidemiology of foodborne illness, while PulseNet focuses on the DNA fingerprinting of disease-causing bacteria. Shortly after the advent of FoodNet, reported outbreaks suddenly doubled; this is almost certainly a reflection of the program's relative muscularity rather than a true increase in contamination.

The advent of PulseNet marked another crucial step forward in the monitoring of foodborne illness. The program is based on a technology known as pulsed-field gel electrophoresis (let's just call it PFGE from here on out, shall we?), a method of DNA analysis that allows epidemiologists to "fingerprint" a specific outbreak's pathogen. With PFGE, researchers can know if a rash of *E. coli* O157:H7 cases in say, Vermont, are connected to the outbreaks in Kansas and Florida. PFGE works because bacteria replicate by splitting in two and because every bacterium is built on a unique genetic makeup. These identifying markers and the technology to interpret them don't do much for anyone who's already eaten the wrong hamburger or spinach salad, but they do provide a degree of traceability—and thus, accountability— long lacking in our complex food-supply chain.

Today, the safety of our food, insomuch as it relates to pathogens, is overseen primarily by a trio of governmental agencies: the United States Department of Agriculture, the Food and Drug Administration, and the CDC. Each plays a role (or a few roles), often through interagency departments that, despite being a fractional component of a larger organization, are themselves large and bureaucratically unwieldy.

That the US government has committed so many resources to combat foodborne illness should come as some relief. I say "should" because the truth is, our food system is so big and so under the purview of for-profit, limited liability corporations that what appears to be a robust regulatory environment is actually severely lacking in its ability and, some would argue, possibly even the will to enforce existing law. A perfect example is the USDA meat inspection program called the Hazard

Analysis and Critical Control Point (HACCP) system, which was launched in 1996 with the intent of modernizing meat inspection and the testing protocol for pathogenic bacteria.

This is all well and good, but the funny thing is, HACCP actually allows many inspection processes to be conducted by the meat companies themselves. Now, I don't know about you, but this has a certain "fox guarding the henhouse" feel that doesn't do a heck of a lot for my confidence. Sure, one could argue that for-profit food producers have a built-in motivation to keep their product safe for human consumption, if not because they actually care about the well-being of their customers (crazy talk, I know) but because they'd prefer to avoid the lawsuits and related bad press that outbreaks can impart.

But here's the thing: The scale, scope, and complexity of the modern-day food system make it very difficult to prove accountability beyond a reasonable doubt, and the producers know this. Even when they are held accountable, the repercussions are often not dire enough to outweigh the added cost of keeping the bacteria out of their products in the first place. In other words, foodborne illness becomes an equation: Spend *this* much to keep the bacteria out of the food in the first place, or spend *this* much cleaning up the fallout from any potential outbreaks.

Sometimes, it seems as if our regulatory agencies take the same view. Indeed, reports have shown that under HACCP, USDA employees have been discouraged from halting production lines, even when they strongly suspect contamination. A leaked USDA memo made it clear that inspectors would be held responsible for stopping production unless there was absolute, irrefutable evidence of contamination. That's a tall order, given the tremendous speed and commotion inherent to the modern slaughterhouse. And speaking strictly as someone who would really rather not spend the rest of his days on dialysis, waiting for a kidney transplant, I'd *much* prefer that the production line be stopped even when there's something less than irrefutable evidence of contamination.

Let's say a USDA or an FDA inspector *does* find contamination, no ifs, ands, or buts. Given the ease with which these bacteria spread in all the commingling of animal bits inside these facilities, surely he or she can order the shutdown of the entire operation, right? Um, no, not quite. Oh, you mean she can demand that only the affected production line be halted? Well, not exactly. But not to fear, it's not as if she's powerless. In fact, upon discovering irrefutable evidence of contamination by pathogenic bacteria in meat headed for the national food supply, the inspector is directed to *consult with the company and advise them about how they should best remedy the situation.* Comforted now?

Meanwhile, the product still flows, and the bacteria still spread along the food industry's complex and far-reaching supply chains. If you think this all sounds so ridiculous, so utterly, impossibly irresponsible to be true, consider that in 2002, the Public Citizen and the Government Accountability Project discovered that even after repeatedly testing positive for salmonella contamination, several (not one, but *several*) ground beef processing facilities were allowed to continue operations for several (again, not one, but *several*) months before action was taken to clean things up.

In any event, through the USDA's Food Safety and Inspection

Service (FSIS), the agency oversees all domestic and imported meat, poultry, milk, and nonshell eggs (those not sold in the shell). In the far corner, responsible for the safety of our domestic and imported fruits, vegetables, seafood, shell eggs, processed dairy (cheese, etc.), and grains, as well as processed foods, is the FDA. If you're worried about the FDA being overworked in its tireless quest to keep you safe from pathogenic bacteria, well, don't be. In fact, the FDA inspects a given facility only *once every 7 years*. But surely they're keeping a careful eye on the food arriving in our harbors, from places such as China, the country from which we now import 60 percent of our apple juice and the country that recently that sickened 300,000 of its own infants with baby formula contaminated by melamine. Surely, they're keeping tabs on that stuff, right? Oh, they are, they are: a whole 1 percent of it. My suggestion: Just be sure that any imported food you eat is part of that 1 percent that gets inspected by the FDA. Oh, wait a second: That's totally impossible. Might as well cross your fingers and keep your health insurance up to date.

To understand why safety-related oversight of our nation's food system can sometimes seem as if it favors the producers rather than the public, it's helpful to examine who, precisely, is tasked with running these agencies. Most recently, consider the July 2009 appointment of Michael Taylor, the Obama administration's food-safety czar. As such, Taylor will be in charge of implementing any food-safety legislation that makes it through Congress. This makes him the singularly most powerful individual in the realm of food safety who is cashing US government paychecks today.

Which in and of itself is no big deal; after all, someone needs to be in charge, and it could be argued that the lack of a figure-head at the top of the food-safety hierarchy has been a detriment to us all. It could also be argued that the appointment of Taylor is indicative of our government's priorities as they pertain to food safety. To wit: Taylor's professional career has been conducted almost entirely through a revolving door between the FDA and Monsanto. For the latter, he served as an attorney through the District of Columbia law firm King & Spaulding before becoming policy chief at the FDA, at a time when the agency was constructing its policy around genetically modified organisms (GMOs). Taylor also oversaw the approval of Monsanto's genetically engineered bovine growth hormone (rBGH/rBST), which was banned in Australia, Canada, Europe, Japan, and New Zealand but has become a cornerstone of the US milk industry, with no labeling required.

Now, the subject of GMOs could fill a book (actually, it already has), but suffice it to say that despite FDA scientists' contending "the processes of genetic engineering and traditional breeding are different, and according to the technical experts in the agency, they lead to different risks," the agency approved genetically modified (GM) foods without any required safety studies. In short, any decision making regarding the safety of these products was left to the corporations producing them. It is important to note that recent studies have demonstrated a causal relationship between GM foods and afflictions such as infertility, asthma, allergies, and dysfunctional insulin regulation (to name but a few) in animals.

In any case, Taylor didn't hang around the FDA for long; in 1994, he slid over to the USDA, where he served as administrator of FSIS and acting undersecretary for food safety. Shortly after, Monsanto came knocking again, and Taylor moved back to the company, where he became vice president for public policy. Which is a really just a fancy way of saying he was a lobbyist.

It would be one thing if Taylor's career path was an anomaly, but it is not. At both the FDA and the USDA, high-level staff members move seamlessly between agricultural corporations, industry trade groups, and the regulatory agencies charged with keeping our nation's food supply safe. Proponents of the revolving door will say that these people have the experience necessary to navigate the complexities of our nation's food system and the related issues. Maybe so, maybe so. But even the neophyte cynic can't help but wonder if perhaps this cozy relationship threatens the impartiality needed to crack down on an industry run amuck and if a culture of corporate favoritism might arise in such an environment.

While the USDA/FSIS and the FDA go about their business of sniffing out pathogenic bacterium before and after it has entered the supply chain, the CDC tracks the spread and, lately, the emergence of the bacterium itself. Remember FoodNet and PulseNet? The CDC doesn't have anything to do with the food itself, but once an outbreak happens, the agency begins the difficult—and often fruitless—task of tracing it to its origin. Think of it this way: If the FSIS and the FDA caught every nasty bug before it slipped into the fast-moving river of our food system, there wouldn't be much need to get the CDC involved at all. Of course, as we know all too well, the FSIS and the FDA aren't exactly batting a thousand.

And so we are faced with a conundrum: Despite PFGE, despite refrigeration and countless other food-related technologies, despite the regulatory oversight of three of our government's largest agencies, despite our general vastly improved understanding of foodborne illness along with our evolving ability to monitor and trace it, the issue of food safety has never felt more urgent and real. The outbreaks are getting bigger and more deadly. The bacteria are evolving, and new strains are emerging. In short, these threats to our public health seem perfectly capable of shrugging off our every attempt to thwart their spread. Which makes it rather hard not to wonder: What are we doing wrong? How can we make our food safe?

To answer this question, I believe we need to look beyond the immediate threat of pathogenic bacteria to the larger trends that have accompanied the rise of foodborne illness in the mainstream of public consciousness. Because at the same time this has happened, the techniques by which we grow, process, and distribute food in this country have evolved, too, in ways that would have been unimaginable only a few decades ago. Consider that we now eat hamburgers made from the fleshy bits of hundreds of cows and adulterated with an ammoniated slurry intended to protect us from the real possibility that any one of those cows—which may have come from different continents— was contaminated with *E. coli* O157:H7. We now have a single peanut butter facility so large that its reach extends to 46 states and the salmonella it disseminates can infect more than 22,000 people. We now are fighting pathogens that only a few years ago were practically unheard of, pathogens that many people believe have arisen not in spite of our modernized food system but *because* of it. At the same time, new research is showing that we now are physically more vulnerable to foodborne illness than at any time in human history, and that this vulnerability is only exacerbated by attempts to scrub the food system of pathogenic bacteria. Attempts that, if the current profit-driven trend toward ever more consolidation holds, will surely fail.

If there is a lesson to be drawn from collective failure to make our food "safer," perhaps it is this: Despite our impressive, ever-improving technologies and increasing vigilance, maybe we are focusing on the wrong things. Perhaps foodborne illness isn't the disease; maybe it's a symptom of a larger, more systemic malaise. And until we begin to address that malaise, we won't know what truly safe food really is.

3

The thrusting of foodborne pathogenic bacteria into the mainstream spotlight is due to numerous factors, but perhaps none so much as the bacterium *Escherichia coli*. *E. coli,* as it's commonly known, was discovered in 1885 by Theodor Escherich, a German-Austrian pediatrician who spent much of his career attempting to reverse the alarmingly high infant mortality rates of the time. With very good reason: Today, the global infant mortality rate is just 7 per 1,000 live births; in 1900, it was almost 2,400 percent higher, at 165 per 1,000.

Given that *E. coli* O157:H7 has become arguably the most feared of all the 200-plus foodborne illnesses (and in remarkably little time; remember, the first widespread outbreak of *E. coli* O157:H7 was barely 30 years ago), it surprised me to learn that it doesn't actually kill very many people: about 60 per year. Both salmonella and listeria kill far more Americans, to the tune of about 500 each, year in, year out. But perhaps because O157:H7 was the bacterium responsible for the outbreak that caused widespread psychological unease regarding the safety of our nation's food supply, or perhaps because O157:H7 has a habit of preying on young children, or perhaps because death by O157:H7 is a particularly nasty affair, or maybe because O157:H7 is widely perceived to be a creation of the modern industrial food system (probably it's a bit of each of these), *E. coli* O157:H7 has become the poster child for 21st-century foodborne illness.

It surprised me to learn that you and I almost certainly have ingested *Escherichia coli* recently; it's even more certain that at this very moment, we have numerous *E. coli* bacteria pinballing around our lower intestines like they own the place. In a sense, they *do* own the place (or, at the very least, rent it), because our intestines have been infested with *E. coli* almost since the day we were born. Newborn babies emerge from the womb with sterile digestive tracts, but within a mere 48 hours, they are colonized by *E. coli*. This may sound rather disconcerting, but in fact the majority of the more than 700 known strains of the *E. coli* bacterium are utterly harmless. You could eat them all day long and not know it. Actually, you do eat them all day long.

What's more, the harmless strains that are currently hurtling through your digestive tract propelled by their flagella (the long, thin, tail-like strands that provide the bacteria's ambulation) are part of the normal, healthy flora of the gut. If that's not enough to make you want to cuddle up to an *E. coli* or two, consider that the bacterium produces vitamin K, which is necessary for blood coagulation, and (get this) helps *prevent the establishment of pathogenic bacteria within the intestine*. In other words, consuming those harmless strains of *E. coli* actually *protects you from bacteria that can make you sick*. Please remember this point, as we'll be touching on it later.

There are four basic subtypes of pathogenic *Escherichia coli*. Most common and deadly is not the type that includes the O157:H7 strain that has dominated US food-safety news headlines; rather, it is a group known as *enterotoxigenic E. coli* (ETEC, if you're into wonky bacteria-related anagrams, and who isn't?). ETEC is commonly called Montezuma's Revenge or "traveler's diarrhea," and I probably don't need to say much more about it, particularly if you've had a little ETEC lodged in your intestine, at which point you most likely got to know your bathroom a whole lot better than you would've preferred. The one thing I will add is this: ETEC is one of the leading causes of infant death worldwide, responsible for about 380,000 premature deaths each year. It's not that the bacterium is so incredibly toxic; the danger is the chronic dehydration that typically accompanies an infection. In the United States, dehydration generally isn't a life-threatening condition. Unfortunately, in much of the world, where medical facilities are often lacking or nonexistent, it very much is.

Next up in our quartet of evil *E. coli* is the enteropathogenic strain (EPEC). Like ETEC, EPEC causes intestinal distress and diarrhea, though it does so through a different mechanism. And like ETEC, it is a major cause of infant mortality in third-world countries.

Number three is enteroinvasive *E. coli* (EIEC), which can cause particularly nasty diarrhea coupled with high fever. It can also severely damage the walls of the intestine. EIEC is generally considered not to be a major threat in the United States; however, because its symptoms are identical to shigellosis, some experts believe it is underreported. The only major known US foodborne outbreak of EIEC occurred in 1973, and it was spread by a batch of cheese imported from France.

Finally, and most relevant to the current landscape of foodborne illness in America, we get to *enterohemorrhagic E. coli* (EHEC), also known as "Shiga toxin–producing *E. coli*" (STEC). The STEC strains of pathogenic *E. coli* include O157:H7, the current bully in the playground of foodborne illness. That's because O157:H7 is at once particularly durable, particularly deadly, and increasingly prevalent in the US food system. This is not a comforting trio of traits, but it is nonetheless true, and it is in no small part the reason why the conversation surrounding food safety in this nation has become so urgent in recent years.

It has been less than three decades since *E. coli* rose to prominence as an instigator of foodborne illness in the United States. It is a rise that was launched by the 1982 outbreak at "Restaurant A" starring STEC and, more specifically, O157:H7. This was the first widespread public appearance by O157:H7 (a retrospective examination of more than 3,000 *E. coli* cultures turned up a single positive sample from 1975), and it provoked a raging debate regarding its origins and, more applicable to our current food-safety policy, how we produce food—in particular, meat—in this country.

Be forewarned: The coming paragraphs are going to feature plenty of poop talk, which is not so much a reflection of my sense of humor (okay, maybe it is, but in my defense, I have two young sons) as the fact that poop is EHEC's preferred medium of growth and host exchange. Specifically, it likes to gather in the excretions of cattle, a species that is unaffected by even the most virulent strains because, like all animals, the cells of cows lack the receptors that allow the toxins in O157:H7 to take hold. This is good for the cows but decidedly inconvenient for us, because O157:H7 colonizes quite nicely in the intestinal tract of bovines, residing primarily in the final few inches that precede daylight. This is called the "terminal rectum". Besides being a great name for an alternative rock band, this is pretty much what it sounds like: the caboose of the bovine digestive system.

It's impossible to know exactly what percentage of the approximately 100 million US cattle harbor O157:H7; a 2003 USDA study found that 13.8 percent of beef cattle and 5.9 percent of dairy cows carried the organism. It also found that O157:H7 was gaining a foothold in other species: 3.6 percent of pigs, 5.2 percent of sheep, and 2.8 percent of goats tested positive. But these findings were based on representative populations, not the entire US herd. Because *E. coli* spreads so readily, it's entirely possible that by now it has infected an even larger percentage of our national livestock population.

In any event, *E. coli*'s path from terminal rectum to your plate isn't a big mystery, particularly when you consider the conditions that prevail at most stockyards and meatpacking facilities, where livestock is raised in direct contact with its feces and that of all its brethren. Out in California's San Joaquin Valley, on my way back to the airport after visiting the largest raw milk dairy in North America (more on that later), I passed the turn to a huge beef operation. I'd never seen one before, so I pulled into the wide dirt lane, half expecting to be apprehended at any moment; somehow, it seemed strange that I'd be allowed to get this close. But no one bothered me, so I continued, driving past yard after yard of penned cattle, their hooves mired in mud and manure and piss. To be honest, they weren't as tightly packed as I'd imagined, and for a moment, I allowed myself to believe that it really wasn't so bad, at least from the standpoint of cleanliness. Then I realized that at some point, presumably, those cattle would need to lie down. And when they did, they'd be reposing in a shallow lagoon of excrement. Perhaps that explained why they were such a uniform shade of brown.

The problem extends further down the supply chain, first to the modern slaughter facilities, where cattle are processed at the rate of about two per minute. If this sounds like a pretty rapid pace to be dispatching, gutting, and skinning 1,500-pound animals, you're right. And if you're wondering if perhaps this is a little too fast to ensure that none of the fecal matter slathered on most of these animals winds up in the finished product . . . well, we already know the answer to that, don't we? The fact is, if you're eating meat from a modern confinement livestock facility, you're almost certainly eating shit. That's not speculation or rhetoric. It's just the truth, and there's really only one other thing to be said: Want some fries with that?

Now, a certain amount of cow manure in your food isn't necessarily going to make you sick (it isn't necessarily going to make your neighbors want come over for burgers on the grill, either). For one thing, you're probably cooking your meat, and if you're cooking it to an internal temperature of at least 155°F, you're putting some major hurt on even the most virulent of the bad guys. And not every piece of meat is going to contain pathogenic bacteria in the first place. That's the good news.

The bad news, at least pertaining to hamburgers and the chances that any particular beef patty is going to make you sick, is that anytime you eat a burger procured from the industrial meat-processing system, you're exposing yourself to numerous animals, any one of which could have been contaminated by O157:H7. Of course, it wasn't always like this: Once upon a time, way back about 30 or so years ago, hamburgers were made from the trimmings and less-choice cuts of a particular animal. In other words, a butcher would break apart an animal, using a certain amount of it for ground beef. Then, he'd move on to the next critter. And so on. In select butcher shops, this is the way it still works. But in your supermarket freezer, where the pre-formed patties are frozen together like chunks of petrified pulpwood, that is decidedly *not* how it works. The overall risk may still be small, but the potentially great number of animals from which each of those burgers is formed magnifies it.

Now, this might simply be a bit disgusting if it weren't for the fact that O157:H7 is a particularly nasty little fellow. Most vexing, it produces a substance known as Shiga toxin, which in addition to having a creepy name is actually one of the most powerful toxins on earth; the CDC has classified it as a potential bioterrorist agent. Shiga toxins bind to your cell walls and eventually work their way into the cell, inhibiting protein synthesis and making you feel really, really crummy.

The other downside of O157:H7 is that it takes only about a dozen microbes of the stuff to make you ill. To put this in context, salmonella doesn't get dangerous until it amasses a billion or so microbes. It's not as if a billion microbes is enough that you can see 'em on your plate, but when only 12 of the suckers can make you good and sick, the margin of error is rather thin.

And if you do end up consuming those 12 or more O157:H7 microbes? Hang on to your hat and head for the loo, because the first symptoms of infection by O157:H7 are generally digestive in nature. You'll probably start off with a bout of severe abdominal cramping, to be followed by an episode of bloody diarrhea. If you're like most folks who contract O157:H7, you'll get away with a relatively brief period of said symptoms and recover quickly. It might take a day or two, and it will probably feel like much longer, but you'll live to eat another burger.

But not everyone will rebound, because in young children, the elderly, or the immune suppressed, O157:H7 can impart a condition known as hemolytic uremic syndrome, aka HUS. This happens to somewhere between 2 and 10 percent of everyone infected by O157:H7 (because it's impossible to know exactly how many people are ever infected, it's impossible to know exactly what percentage of cases lead to HUS). The most recent studies put the HUS mortality rate at 4.6 percent. *E. coli* O157:H7 without HUS can still cause death, but the mortality rate is quite low: In children under age 5, one of the most vulnerable populations, it's 0.3 percent.

Death isn't the only undesirable outcome. A nasty case of HUS can pretty much wipe out your kidneys, consigning you to a life of dialysis and perhaps even necessitating a kidney transplant. It can cause stroke, seizures, coma, and paralysis. In short, HUS can bum you out in a very big way and radically alter the course of your life.

Given all of this, it's a little disconcerting to consider that only a few decades ago, O157:H7 wasn't even part of the food-safety conversation. The first known outbreak was less than 30 years ago, and it would be another 11 years before Jack in the Box made the bacterium a household name. To put this in perspective, consider that in just the first 6 months of 2010, there were over a half-dozen O157:H7 outbreaks in the United States. All of which begs the question: Where did *E. coli* O157:H7 come from? And to play on the classic Grateful Dead bumper sticker, why does it keep following us around?

To understand why, you need to know a bit about human biology. Specifically, you need to know that the human stomach is a very acidic environment, where pH levels typically range between 1.5 and 3.5 (the lower the pH, the more acidic the environment; a pH of 7 is considered neutral). There are five walls in the human stomach; the innermost layer, the mucosa, manufactures stomach acid, most of which is of the hydrochloric variety. Most of us have somewhere between a tablespoon and a cup of the stuff sloshing around in our bellies. From a foodborne-illness perspective, this is a particularly good thing, since the acidic nature of the human gut presents a hurdle to many pathogenic bacteria, which typically can't survive when the pH drops below 5.0 or so. But *E. coli* O157:H7 is unusually resistant to our stomach acid; a certain percentage of the bacteria can survive the shock of the human hydrochloric acid bath and make their way to the intestine, where all hell breaks loose.

It is precisely this resistance that has provoked debate over the origins of O157:H7 and the way in which we feed livestock in the modern industrial meat-production system. Much of this debate can be traced to a report in a September 1998 edition of *Science*—a report authored by Francisco Diez-Gonzalez, Todd Callaway, Menas Kizoulis, and James Russell. The authors concluded that cattle fed primarily on grain (as are most beef cattle living in Concentrated Animal Feeding Operations, or CAFO) had lower stomach pH.

See, cattle weren't designed to eat grain; their digestive system does just fine on grass and hay, but throw enough starch at it, and it's simply unable to complete the digestion process. This means that a certain amount of the grain makes its way to the colon undigested, where it ferments and produces acids. According to the researchers of the *Science* study, this acidic environment encourages the *E. coli* that naturally resides in the colon to develop acid resistance. And thus a rural legend was born: *E. coli* O157:H7 is a product of our habit of feeding corn to cattle, a practice that is less than a century old and conveniently fits the timeline of O157:H7's rise to pathogenic prominence. It's a theory that has persisted and is often held up by the growing legion of grass-based meat producers, who raise their animals on pasture and hay, rather than commercial grain rations.

The only problem: The theory is probably wrong. "I wish we had been right, because it sure makes for a neat story," Todd Callaway told me when I called him up at his lab in Texas, where he spends an awful lot of his time studying and thinking about *E. coli*. Indeed, the more Callaway researched the issue of O157:H7 and its relation to a grain-based diet, the more uncertain he became. "Sometimes we'd find that grain increased the number of O157:H7, and sometimes we'd find it decreased it.

We do think there's a possible connection to feed, but we can't get a grip on what it is."

And, says Callaway, it's increasingly looking as if O157:H7 has been around for a lot longer than anyone thought. "Basically, what we have is a normal strain of *E. coli* that just happens to have imported some genes from *Shigella* 50,000 years ago. And it hasn't really changed since. I think what happened is there were so many other diseases around that it sort of got lost. But now we've knocked a lot of those down, and then we had a few cases of O157:H7 pop up, and now everyone's looking for it. If you're out there looking for it, especially with these new molecular technologies we have, you're going to find it."

None of which is to say that Callaway dismisses the threat posed by O157:H7. "I've been working with this stuff for more than a decade, and I'm always paranoid that I'm going to take it home to my family," he told me. "It didn't evolve to attack humans, but it's a real survivor. It's tolerant of the sun, and it can survive in aerobic or anaerobic environments. If there's no protein around, it can ferment sugar. Not many bugs can do that." He sounded slightly in awe of the stuff, but to be honest, I was kind of ready for him to shut up; he was beginning to scare me a little.

"Nope," he continued, in his soft Texas twang, "it's not a true human pathogen, in the sense that it's not hunting us or using us to spread. We're just collateral damage, really." This I did not find tremendously comforting. He turned back to the issue of feed. "I do think there's something with the feed. We've always known that changing the diet in cattle affects their gut population. Maybe it's that the rest of the gut population is changing, allowing O157 to survive. Because that's what it likes to do: Survive. It's a survivor."

It actually gets worse, because in recent years another half-dozen strains of enterohemorrhagic *E. coli* have emerged as threats. The strains are known as O26, O45, O111, O121, O145, and O103 and, according to the CDC, are collectively responsible for approximately 30 deaths in the United States annually. Or perhaps many more: Because only about 5 percent of US labs have the capacity to test for these strains in human fecal samples, it is impossible to know exactly how pervasive they've become and how many deaths they are truly causing.

And are likely to cause for some time, because the USDA does not current classify these strains as "adulterants," which is the official designation required to mandate testing by meat processors. This was once the case with O157:H7, too, although the firestorm that followed the Jack in the Box outbreak provoked the political will necessary to override the meat industry's self-interested objections and declare the strain an adulterant. This was important not only because it laid the groundwork necessary to implement widespread testing but also because the Federal Safety and Inspection Service's power to seek (but not demand) recalls is limited to those products that have been deemed adulterated.

What might be the holdup in classifying these strains as adulterants? In no small part, it is due to efforts by the meat industry to escape further regulation. In a letter to Secretary of Agriculture Tom Vilsack dated August 18, 2010, the American

Meat Institute's (AMI) J. Patrick Boyle stated that "the designation of non-O157:H7 STECs as adulterants will result in a misdirected regulatory program that will cause more harm than good." It's not entirely clear if Boyle was speaking of the potential harm to American consumers or to the institute's members, which produce about 95 percent of the meat consumed in this country. But I'm willing to make a guess.

Boyle also noted that "no non-O157:H7 STEC illness outbreaks have been confirmed in the US" and, therefore, that "given the absence of non-O157:H7 STEC illness outbreaks linked to beef, it is not readily apparent that there is an equally compelling reason to declare non-O157:H7 STECs as adulterants under present circumstances."

Strictly speaking, Boyle was correct, but only by 10 days: On August 28, Cargill Meat Solutions recalled 8,500 pounds of beef products that carried E. coli O26 after three people in two states fell ill. It was the first recall of O26-contaminated ground beef in this country.

The O26 outbreak certainly didn't come as a surprise to foodborne-illness attorney Bill Marler (you'll meet him later), who'd already doled out a half-million bucks to have Mansour Samadpour, a Seattle based microbiologist who specializes in foodborne pathogens, test 5,000 samples of ground beef. The result: About 2 percent of the beef tested positive for non-O157 STECs. "It is less prevalent than O157," Samadpour told me when I called him. "The incidence rate is lower than O157. But it is definitely out there, and it can cause death just like O157. You don't have to wait for someone to die to start testing for it."

I didn't mention that Samadpour's observation was already a little late.

Samadpour contends that the AMI's resistance to the adulterant labeling has less to do with the industry's lack of desire for more regulation and instead hinges on what he believes will be the inevitable outcome. "The testing is not that big a deal, okay? But will they need to reject more product? Of course. Will it result in increased costs? Of course."

To which I can only add: Would the vast majority of American meat consumers, most of whom have no idea just how much STEC-contaminated meat is currently being sold, want the non-O157 strains labeled as adulterants? Of course.

4

The Columbia Center in downtown Seattle is a tall building, rising 937 feet and 76 stories above ground level, although another seven stories are sunk into the earth below the pavement. It is the tallest building in the Pacific Northwest; including its subterranean holdings, it is the building with the most total stories (83) west of the Mississippi. It is not where I would have expected my quest to parse America's food-safety landscape to take me, but it is nonetheless where I ended up on a warm, overcast morning in the second week of June 2010.

I should preface this by mentioning that during my early reporting, one name kept popping up: Bill Marler. "Have you heard of Bill Marler?" people would say. Or: "You should really talk to Bill Marler." Or: "Bill Marler is a crook." (To be honest, this happened only once.) My interest was piqued; clearly, I needed to know more about this fellow.

As it turned out, this wasn't hard to do, because William Marler, Esq., is a man in possession of a substantial Internet presence. The law firm he founded with Bruce Clark in 1998 is known as (appropriately enough) Marler Clark, and it maintains no fewer than 32 Web sites and blogs relating to foodborne illness and food safety in general. Actually, by now there are probably more, but at the time I visited the Marler Clark offices on the 66th floor of the Columbia Center, 32 was the number, a number that seems to me entirely adequate to make the point that, at least in regards to the foodborne-illness Internet landscape, Marler Clark rules the roost.

Of course, this is not an entirely altruistic pursuit. It is safe to say that Marler Clark is the most prominent and successful foodborne-illness litigation firm in the world, and it is safe to say that Bill Marler is the most experienced and knowledgeable foodborne-illness attorney at his firm. Ergo, and no one I've spoken with disputes this, Bill Marler is the leading foodborne-illness litigator on earth. If you are sickened by pathogenic bacteria in food, believe that you can prove your case, and furthermore would like to be handsomely compensated for your suffering, you should probably give Bill a call.

Given his prominence in his field, I'd expected some difficulty reaching Marler by phone and a greater challenge arranging a face-to-face meeting. As it turned out, the former was exceedingly simple; only a few hours after I left a message on his voice mail, Bill Marler called me back.

Over my years of journalistic reporting, I've come to be somewhat leery of using lawyers, and in particular trial lawyers, as sources. They are typically not unbiased and, just as typically, are quite skilled at spinning a story in whichever direction best suits their professional pursuits. Many would say Bill Marler is no different, and that may well be true. Actually, I'm certain that it is true. But it is hard to deny that the man knows more about the issues of food safety and foodborne illness from more viewpoints than perhaps anyone, anywhere. He is a walking, talking encyclopedia of the history, symptoms, causes, and possible solutions to our nation's food-safety and foodborne-illness crisis. For a time, he was on the short list to fill the position of undersecretary of food safety in the Obama administration but was passed over because, according to him, he's "not controllable enough." "I don't have the need to burnish my résumé so I can get a job at ConAgra after my term," Marler told me, looking exceedingly proud.

Despite my early reluctance to use a trial lawyer as a source and my enduring suspicion that his occupation can't help but color his view of food-safety landscape (but then, couldn't that be said about anyone?), I began to enjoy talking with Marler. I came to value his perspective on the workings of our food system. He is extremely charming, maintaining a direct, folksy tone that rarely comes off as preachy, a combination that gives an impression of candidness. He peppers his speech with curses, though I have little doubt that he knows exactly when and where to exchange the vulgarity for more formal language. Marler does not come across as arrogant or combative, although he can surely be both. He exudes a high level of energy in general and, more specifically, exceptional passion for the subject of food safety—passion he does not let get in the way of a finely honed sense of humor. When I asked him what he does to protect himself from foodborne pathogens, he said, "I drink a lot of scotch."

Bill Marler's path to a corner office on the 66th floor of the Columbia Center and a professional life that has provided him with the qualifications for such a position was circuitous and marked by the sort of progress that only seems like progress in hindsight. For instance (and bear with me here), one significant turning point hinged on a $900 Ford Pinto.

This was in 1992, when Marler was an ambitious but largely unknown lawyer working at a huge Seattle firm. He'd caught a nice break (or more likely worked his way into one) and was assigned a high-profile case representing two families whose kids had been murdered by a state parolee named Westley Allan Dodd. Dodd was a savage and twisted fellow, having killed three children following his early release from prison and tucked one of the bodies in his closet for long-term storage. Apparently, this wasn't enough to satisfy Dodd's bloodlust, so he slunk into a movie theater, snatched another child, and fled in his Pinto, for which he'd paid—you guessed it—900 bucks.

Now, any Ford Pinto is subject to fits of unreliability, and Dodd's was no different. With kidnapped child in transit and pursuers close on Dodd's heels, it promptly broke down, leaving him at the mercy of the law. Dodd was captured, his victim was released, and Marler's case against the state for gross negligence in releasing the murderer early was a lock. "I went from hardworking obscurity to people knowing I had this big case in my pocket," recalled Marler, and I sensed a twinge of nostalgia in his tone.

After his success with the Dodd trial, Bill Marler was perfectly positioned within his firm for the assignment of another high-profile case, and that case just happened to be the 1993 *E. coli* outbreak at the Jack in the Box restaurant chain. It was, Marler told me, a "perfect storm" of foodborne-illness awareness and suffering. For starters, the pathogen in question wasn't merely *E. coli* but that particularly deadly variant, O157:H7. Jack in the Box wasn't the first O157:H7 outbreak in the United States; that dubious honor belongs to a 1982 incident that sickened people in Oregon and Michigan who'd eaten at "restaurant A" (commonly known to be McDonald's). But it was the largest outbreak thus far, and it came at a time when numerous strategies, technologies, and media outlets were converging to drive awareness of foodborne pathogens and the manner in which they are disseminated throughout our food system.

"This happened just as molecular technology was coming up," Marler explained to me. "We were beginning to be able to identify and trace these pathogens with some accuracy and efficiency." He was talking about pulsed field gel electrophoresis (PFGE), the pathogen-fingerprinting technology that had been invented less than a decade earlier. Another factor: an evolving business model that increasingly depended on mass-produced food being distributed in multiple franchises, in multiple jurisdictions, often with disparate rules and regulations. Indeed, the Jack in the Box outbreak came shortly after the state of Washington, following a small O157:H7 incident at a nursing home in Walla Walla, had mandated that the internal temperature of hamburgers be 155°F, an increase of 15 degrees from the previous mandate of 140°F (*E. coli* O157:H7 can't survive temperatures higher than 155°F).

But Jack in the Box chose to ignore the new law. "Here's the dilemma: You're a national food chain working under a code that tells you you've got to cook your hamburgers to 140 degrees.

And then some wild-ass state up near Canada decides it's gotta be 155." Marler chuckled, and I wondered if it wasn't because this very dilemma—and how Jack in the Box chose to resolve it—had played a large role in making him a wealthy man. He continued: "Long story short, Jack in the Box decides it's too difficult to hit 155 with a 2-minute cook time. And so they decided to stick with a 2-minute cook time." In other words, the Jack in the Box operating practices meant O157:H7 would emerge uncomfortably toasty but largely unscathed from the restaurant chain's griddles nationwide.

In any event, Marler, with his post-Wesley Alan Dodd cache as rising star, was awarded the Jack-in-the-Box case, and embarked on a quest to become an instant expert in all things E. Coli. At the time, there simply weren't that many experts on the issue of pathogenic bacteria in food, and Marler soon rose to the fore of the issue. "The harder you work, the more you know, and the better you do. I've found that to be a fairly easy way to get ahead in life," he told me. Also, he says, the birth of his first daughter in 1992 strongly impacted his worldview as it relates to food borne illness (after all, many of the Jack-in-the-Box victims were children, and youngsters continue to be among those most afflicted by pathogenic bacteria, owing to their nascent immune systems). "It didn't take much for me to go home and say 'oh my goodness, this could happen to us.'"

Of course, Marler is well aware that some people will view his motivations through the stereotypical lens of the ambulance-chasing lawyer, a view that is arguably brought into sharper focus by the nature of foodborne illness outbreaks. Given the scale and scope of our modern, industrialized food system, a serious event can be spread across multiple states, and affect dozens, if not tens of thousands of consumers, each of which might stand to collect millions of dollars. While most personal injury lawyers chase their income one car crash at a time, an attorney specializing in foodborne illness can realize the earning power of dozens, if not hundreds, of car crashes with a single outbreak. With a typical contingency fee (the amount a lawyer collects if the judgment is favorable to his client) for a trial lawyer running 33 $\frac{1}{3}$%, it's not hard to see how the money can add up.

Marler doesn't deny this, and admits to no small amount of internal turmoil regarding his chosen profession. "There's a big chunk of me that thinks 'wow, I'm making so much money off these horribly sick people.' So do I feel conflicted? Absolutely. I feel very conflicted, and I deal with it the way anybody would: by feeling guilty and then trying to do something good." In Marler's case, this means almost constant lobbying in favor of greater governmental oversight, as well as a seemingly unending string of pro-bono appearances before trade groups and non-profit organizations to share his encyclopedic knowledge and experience.

Marler wrapped up his Jack in the Box work in 1996 and again began taking standard trial lawyer fare: car crashes, crane collapses, train wrecks—basically any unfortunate episode where a plausible line could be drawn between negligence and misery. "I'd made a name for myself as one of the go-to trial lawyers in the Northwest," Marler told me. "I had no shortage of work. It wasn't like I was sitting around thinking, 'Oh, I guess I'll be a foodborne-illness lawyer.'" Still, Marler's no fool, and he kept a keen eye on the foodborne-illness landscape.

It didn't take long for that landscape to bear fruit, and I mean that almost literally, because the next big foodborne-illness case Marler tackled was an outbreak of *E. coli* O157:H7–contaminated apple juice distributed by Odwalla. Marler successfully represented several children who contracted HUS and suffered permanent kidney damage after drinking the contaminated juice. This was a turning point for Marler, who rather presciently recognized that the issue of foodborne illness was not going away and, in fact, was likely to grow like metastatic cancer. "After Odwalla, I went to my partners and said, 'I want to focus on foodborne illness.' And they were like, 'That's a dumb idea.'" Marler guffawed, and who could blame him for relishing their shortsightedness? His guffaw was simply a small piece of the last laugh, which has been going on for over a decade and shows no signs of abating.

Given the recalcitrance of his former partners, Marler struck out on his own, forming Marler Clark with Bruce Clark and Denis Stearns in 1998. The latter had represented Jack in the Box during Marler's pursuit of fiscal justice, and Marler had gained a wily adversary's respect for Stearns's talents. Still, it was a risky move. "They had no business, and I only had a handful. We were definitely out on a limb." But pretty soon, some kids at a local grade school got sick and tested positive for *E. coli* O157:H7, and Marler Clark was no longer out on a limb.

These days, Marler Clark maintains a workforce of eight attorneys and 25 supporting staffers, including a full-time epidemiologist. The firm's grasp on the foodborne-illness litigation landscape is nothing short of dominant: During the 2006 *E. coli* spinach outbreak, Marler Clark represented 105 of 110 total claimants. Bill Marler has proven exceptionally adept at promoting his firm and himself; his primary blog, marlerblog.com, is often updated multiple times daily and receives over one million hits annually. It features heartrending and keenly produced video clips, mostly of clients whose lives have been permanently altered by foodborne illness. He has also proven a quick study in guerilla marketing: In October 2009, Marler Clark sent all 100 US senators a press release urging them to "pass meaningful food-safety legislation by Thanksgiving." The press release was wrapped in a T-shirt that featured a photo of Marler with a thick red line struck across his face. The tagline: Put a Trial Lawyer out of Business.

Marler seems to be an indiscriminate thorn in the side of food producers big and small, with a particular affinity for jockeying with the raw milk crowd, which he views as naive regarding the dangers of their favorite beverage. (Marler actually grew up on a farm, where he butchered pigs, chickens, and rabbits and on occasion drank raw milk.) He travels almost constantly, addressing the Grocery Manufacturers Association or lecturing at a law school or attending a hearing in Washington, DC. His renown and affluence have afforded him a position of power in both his firm and the broader panorama of food safety, and he uses that position to its full advantage.

I met Bill Marler in the lobby of the Columbia Center. I recognized him immediately from his Web site photos but was surprised at his attire, which was casual in the extreme. He wore an untucked button-down short-sleeve shirt, topped by a fleece vest. Below, his bare legs emerged from a pair of khaki-colored shorts, and his feet were clad in running shoes. It wasn't terribly warm outside, nor had he just completed an athletic endeavor; it's just that Bill Marler likes to dress casually, and, therefore, he does. "It's good to be the boss," he told me, with a good-natured chuckle. He struck me as the sort of fellow who'd just parked a big Mercedes; imagine my disappointment to learn that he drives a VW Beetle, disappointment that was mitigated somewhat when I learned he'd fitted it with a vanity plate that reads: ECOLI.

We rode a wood-paneled elevator to the headquarters of Marler Clark, where Marler keeps an office that boasts expansive views of downtown Seattle and Elliott Bay, and of Bainbridge Island, where he lives with his wife and three children. From Marler's office looking north, I could see the Space Needle. I rather enjoyed realizing that I was observing it from a perspective that not many visitors to Seattle are afforded: I was looking down on it.

Marler settled in behind his desk, a table of rough-hewn barn board that was both rustic and classy. He is not a particularly large man, but he is tending toward fleshy in a way that suggests an ample supply of good food and an appetite to match (he is a regular at Bainbridge farmers' markets and keeps a vegetable garden as well as a small flock of laying hens). Behind him and slightly to his right, a gift from a client: a wild boar's head mounted to an interior wall. There were three computers in the office, although the desktop was neat and uncluttered. Sitting across from Marler, I had the best view in the room, although the sight of Marler's head protruding into the sky behind him (naturally, the exterior walls were glass) lent a disembodied feel to his presence that was slightly unsettling. It was almost as if he were a celestial being, and I couldn't help but wonder if he was perfectly aware of this effect.

At the time of my visit, Marler was in the throes of battle with the "raw milkers" (his term). Over the preceding months, I'd kept a bemused eye on the exchanges between Marler and regular commentators at thecompletepatient.com, a blog run by David Gumpert, author of *The Raw Milk Revolution*. Not surprisingly, Gumpert is a proponent and consumer of raw milk, and the regular commentators to his blog are passionate supporters of raw milk and food rights in general. In spite of this (or perhaps because of it), Marler had waded into the fray and become a frequent commenter on Gumpert's blog. This was a little surprising, given that Marler had represented the families of the children whose illnesses had been epidemiologically linked to raw milk. In other words, to Gumpert's followers, he was the enemy, intent on bringing down raw milk dairymen and -women and grinding American's food rights into the dust of an industrial dairy barnyard.

This dynamic had spawned reams of colorful commentary on both the part of Marler ("your mind must be so small that a thimble hat falls around your ears") and a variety of commentators ("you whine and cry to Gumpert when I refer to you and your ambulance-chasing cronies as what you are . . . Bottom Feeding Pond Scum") and eventually led Marler to launch his own Web site, realrawmilkfacts.com. The home page features numerous videos of Marler Clark clients explaining how and to what extent raw milk had sickened them. The heading above the videos reads: REAL LIFE DANGERS OF RAW MILK.

It seemed apparent to me that Marler's site was as much about getting the last word as it was about disseminating the gospel truth regarding raw milk, but either way, it couldn't be denied that the months immediately preceding my trip to Seattle had been particularly bad for raw milk and, therefore, if one were keeping score, particularly good for Bill Marler. A flurry of outbreaks connected to different dairies in multiple states had resulted in numerous illnesses, including one that hospitalized a young Minnesota child sickened by *E. coli* O157:H7. Meanwhile, the Organic Valley Family of Farms cooperative, one of the nation's largest purchasers of fluid organic milk intended for pasteurization and mass market, announced it would terminate the contract of any of its members found to be selling raw milk direct to consumers. With the dairy industry reeling from the recession, many small-scale dairy farms had taken to selling raw milk directly off the farm, collecting anywhere from $5 to $15 per gallon, rather than the approximate $3 per gallon they received from Organic Valley. And, in March 2010, Whole Foods Market had pulled raw milk from the shelves of its stores in the states of California, Connecticut, Pennsylvania, and Washington.

To me, it all added up to a sense that 2010 had the potential to be something of a tipping point for raw milk and, therefore, food rights in general. And as of my visit to Bill Marler's office, it looked to be tipping in a direction that wasn't particularly favorable to the raw milkers. For his part, Marler wasn't quite gloating, but he wasn't far from it. "They've had nine fuckin' outbreaks since January," he told me, waving his arms in the air for emphasis. "Hell, even the meat industry on its worst day doesn't have that."

Despite his disdain for raw milk (which he believes should be legal, but only under strict regulation) and his online quarreling with its devotees, Marler is actually a strident advocate of small-scale, decentralized food systems and believes that the greatest risk factor for the cultivation and distribution of pathogenic bacteria is the sheer enormity of the corporatized, industrial food system. "If you look at the major outbreaks over the years, all of it was mass-produced food. In 16 years of doing this work, I've never sued a local farmer." He paused a moment and then, unable to leave a good dig undug, added, "Well, except for raw milk."

In Marler's view, the industrial model, while being very effective at cranking out large quantities of food for relatively little money, suffers from a perilous side effect. "The scale is so big, every little problem becomes amplified. You don't have two people getting sick; you have 200. Or 2,000." Or, in the case of the Peanut Corporation of America, 22,000. And, because a lot of modern food products—even basic ingredients, such as hamburger—are amalgamated from dozens, if not hundreds, of sources, the potential for cross-contamination is extremely high.

Consider the hamburger that sickened and ultimately paralyzed Stephanie Smith (yes, Smith is a Marler Clark client), who was 22 and a children's dance instructor when she ate the fateful beef patty in the fall of 2007. A front-page investigation in the October 4, 2009, *New York Times* revealed that Smith's frozen, preformed burger, which was processed and distributed by Cargill under the label "American Chef's Selection Beef Patties," had numerous points of origin, including Nebraska, Texas, South Dakota, and Uruguay. Without realizing it— indeed, surely without wanting to—Ms. Smith was partaking of international fare. And given that each of the facilities that supplied the components of her burger processes thousands of animals per day, by eating a single hamburger she was consuming the flesh of countless bovine.

She was also dining on a product that was far more complex than its list of ingredients, which included only the word "beef," suggested. In fact, most mass-produced hamburgers in this country contain much more than simple ground beef. In addition to fillers and flavorings like bread crumbs and spices, Ms. Smith's burger was constructed in part from a product its supplier, Beef Products, terms "fine lean textured beef." Which sounds pretty good, until you realize that fine lean textured beef is rendered from the fatty trimmings that remain after a carcass is processed. As reported by the *New York Times* story, which was awarded a 2010 Pulitzer Prize, the trimmings are heated, run through a centrifuge, and treated with ammonia to kill *E. coli*. The company reportedly cranks out seven million pounds per week of the mashlike substance, which is sold in frozen blocks. I'm not sure about you, but that's not exactly what I picture when I hear the term "fine lean textured beef." Though I suppose the word *textured* should be something of a tip-off; after all, when's the last time your local butcher tried to sell you "textured" beef?

The outbreak that struck down Stephanie Smith was estimated to have sickened 940 people, though none so profoundly as her, and it underscores Marler's points about the dangers inherent to a food system run chiefly on the tenets of cost cutting and efficiency of scale (by using various trimmings products from disparate sources, Cargill managed to save approximately 25 percent in comparison to the cost of burger ground from whole pieces of beef). The meat industry is particularly susceptible, given that the very nature of the product demands that it be raised in proximity to feces. This is compounded by the conditions at the CAFOs that dominate the meat industry, where animals are kept in extremely close quarters, in constant and direct contact with the manure of hundreds, if not thousands, of feedlot mates. "Somewhere, somehow, the wheels just came off the meat industry," Marler told me. "It's degrading to our bodies, to our environment, and to the animals. It's degrading to our morals." I straightened a little in my chair: Had he just said that the way we raise our food is degrading to our morals? By gum, he had.

Contracting *E. coli* O157:H7 was obviously a turning point (and not for the better) in Stephanie Smith's life. But as dramatic and tragic as its ramifications have been and will continue to be, in at least one regard—albeit a morbid one—Smith was lucky: Her case was relatively easy to litigate.

This is not usually the case. Indeed, the factors that determine whether or not Marler Clark will represent a client constitute a list that is both wide reaching and long. I'd sort of assumed that a person with Bill Marler's exceptional knowledge and skills relating to foodborne-illness litigation would be able to spin gold out of practically any gastric disturbance that walked through his door. Heck, on the day I visited him, I was experiencing a bit of travel-related indigestion, and I couldn't help but wonder if perhaps Marler could help me lay the blame for my discomfort at the door of some ginormous food conglomerate. I'd been emitting embarrassing belches all morning, which I'd been uncomfortably suppressing in Marler's office. It seemed only reasonable that I demand compensation for my pain and suffering.

Turns out, it's not quite that simple. First, Marler must consider the incubation period of pathogenic bacteria—the time that passes between its entry into your digestive tract and the moment it starts kicking down your door (so to speak). Now, for most foodborne illness, there's a pretty broad range of incubation; *E. coli* O157:H7 can range from 1 to 10 days, while salmonella poisoning typically rears its ugly head within 48 hours. But Marler regularly hears tales of illness that came on within a few minutes or hours of eating a particular food. He invariably turns down these claims, because none of the bacteria that have garnered favorable settlements for his clients have incubation periods that can be measured in a handful of hours. One of the ironies—and arguably the greatest challenge—of drawing a straight line between a particular illness and a particular meal is that the food that seems most logically guilty simply by its proximity to the onset of symptoms will almost never be the food that actually made you sick.

The lack of straight-line logic extends into the area of smell and taste, because most bacteria do neither, which means that just because you ate a funky-smelling taco salad and got sick 3 days later, it was not necessarily the salad that made you ill. Which is not to say that either Bill Marler or I recommend consuming funky-smelling taco salads; only that smell and taste are poor predictors of your success in regards to compensation.

What gets Marler excited about an individual claim isn't so much the gritty details of that claim (though they are important) but the backdrop against which it is brought to his attention.

Marler is much more likely to consider a claim that happens in the context of an investigation by a regional health department. That's because in most cases, a human sample that tests positive for a common foodborne illness will trigger a report to the local health authorities, who will then follow up with an investigation. There are all sorts of factors that determine how vigorous this investigation will be, but for the purposes of litigation, it doesn't matter so much that it is particularly vigorous, only that it is documented.

The beauty of these investigations is that in a sphere where guilt is difficult to prove, the conclusions of a health department are about as close to a smoking gun as exists. Epidemiologists typically require 95-percent proof before signing their name to a particular conclusion; Marler likes to point out that this is a significantly higher degree of certainty than is required of a jury (51 percent), and that it's really only possible due to the advent of technologies like PFGE. Of course, this standard can just as easily work against a client: If, after conducting an investigation, the health department cannot confirm the source of an outbreak, the case is pretty much dead in the water.

Actually, there is an exception to this rule: A history of accusations, violations, or other health-related incidents against a particular producer can turn the tide in favor of Marler and his client. This history is sometimes the only "evidence," because by the time the investigation has run its course, the offending food has already been disseminated, leaving nothing to trace the bacteria back to. It's sort of like following the rainbow to its end and not finding the pot of gold. But if Marler can generate enough circumstantial evidence, either historical or in the form of improper handling techniques, he stands a good chance of earning a favorable settlement. In one hamburger-based O157:H7 case from 2001, health officials weren't able to find even a trace of the bacterium at the suspected restaurant. But the joint had a record of warnings from the health department and, as it turned out, a flawed cooking method that could allow *E. coli* to survive. Marler dug up this information and bingo: settlement reached.

Of course, meat is not the only point of entry for pathogenic bacteria in our food system. The past few years have seen widespread outbreaks associated with peanuts, spinach, strawberries, and bean sprouts. The irony is that foods that have been heavily processed—in other words, foods that are typically the least nutritious—are least likely to harbor pathogenic bacteria. The processing itself, which usually involves the application of extreme heat, often kills the bacterium that can cause acute illness. The long-term chronic disease that is so often the result of eating these foods is another matter. Still, given the nature of many of the foods implicated in recent widespread recalls, one can only wonder what's next. Tofu and bran flakes, perhaps?

Despite the disparate sources of foodborne illness, most outbreaks share a commonality: They're enormously difficult to trace. PFGE can tell us if disease clusters are related, but the test can't tell us precisely where that disease originated or where the ingredients from that source point are headed. And this brings us to another problematic aspect inherent to our globalized, multiple-source-point food system. The supply chain is simply too convoluted to follow with any certainty. This does two things: First, it makes it very, very difficult to determine with absolute confidence where an outbreak began. Tracing the origin can take weeks or even months; in the meantime, the contaminated product is fanning out across the country, in trucks and trailers and trains, to outlets that can range from local deli to supermarket to burger franchise. Couple the traceability issue with the fact that the incubation period for many foodborne illnesses can be measured in weeks, and you've got a real puzzle on your hands. I mean, can you tell me everything you ate 2 weeks ago and where it came from? No? How about 2 days ago? Me, neither.

As Marler explains it, the best way to understand the system is to visualize a funnel. Up at the top, at the wide end, you've got trillions and trillions of pathogenic bacteria attaching themselves to the foodstuff of their choosing. We'll call this the "outbreak." From there, the outbreak spreads across the supply chain associated with the given food; in modern America, this almost always means crossing numerous state boundaries. And here is a very important point: *Each state has its own protocol for tracking and tracing disease outbreaks.* There is little to no cooperation between states, and there is no such thing as standardized pathogen tracking. "If you look at it historically, you'd say, 'Shit, there's an awful lot of foodborne illness in Minnesota, and not much in Texas,'" Marler told me. "But it's just that Texas is a red state, and red states don't place a priority on public health." Marler is an unapologetic Democrat and huge Obama supporter, so we'll ignore the political dig. Which is fine, because that's not the point anyway. The point is this: Texas and Minnesota take very different approaches to tracking and investigating outbreaks of foodborne illness. And because the

CDC relies on individual states to identify patterns of disease, protocol discrepancies between states are a huge barrier to accurate and timely tracking.

Back to our funnel analogy. By now, our pathogen has spread and is finding its way into the retail food system, perhaps at restaurants, perhaps at supermarkets; very possibly at both. Some folks who purchase the contaminated products will get sick; some won't, either because their immune systems are strong enough to fend off the invader or because they've cooked the product to a high enough temperature to kill the offending bacteria. Some who get sick will become only slightly ill and never associate their discomfort with their food; some will get sicker than that but recover and move on, having not sought treatment. Finally, nearing the narrow end of the funnel will be those who get sick enough (or are fretful enough) to seek medical assistance. And of these, some will be dismissed without being tested for pathogenic bacteria. Of those that are tested, some might receive false assurances (remember the six non-O157 pathogenic strains of *E. coli?*). The ones that do return positive results are the cases emerging from the funnel. These are the cases that are ultimately uploaded to PulseNet, the CDC's outbreak-tracking database. These are the cases that will define the geographical parameters for the ensuing investigation. These are the cases that have a chance of making it to Bill Marler's desk.

The problem (well, not the only problem, but certainly one of the major ones) is that the funnel gets rid of an awful lot of accountability. So much happens between the actual contamination and the positive tests that emerge from the narrow end that it's difficult to figure out where the bacteria entered the system. Which means it's pretty darn difficult to assign blame. Accountability can be thrown off by the wildly disparate ways in which local and state health departments monitor potential outbreaks. Or it can be thrown off by the complexity of the food system itself. Or the lab's ability (or inability) to test for certain pathogens. Or the fact that animals don't always shed the bacteria that make people sick, so that a cow that might test positive for O157:H7 one day, might test negative the next. The more you look, the more you become aware just how circuitous a journey it is through the funnel, with all sorts of blind corners, blocked exits, and shuttered views.

"One of the things the locavore people really have right is the accountability issue," noted Marler, when I commented on the challenge of assigning blame. "I mean, just because you can shake the hand of the guy who sold you your dinner doesn't mean he's not going to poison you. But it does mean you'll know where to find him if he does."

As Marler and I talked, and I began to better understand how outbreaks happen and how they are resolved, I found myself becoming more and more discouraged. It was beginning to sound as if there were no real solutions to this morass of a food system we've created and the risks that seem to simply be a part of the puzzle. Perhaps, I thought, we just need to learn to accept a certain amount of disease and illness. Perhaps we simply need to accept the fact that we don't have the right to eat as we wish. After all, more than 40,000 people die in car crashes every year in the United States, and we're still zooming up and down the highways. Maybe pathogenic bacteria in our food are an unfortunate reality that can't be escaped; maybe the thousands of people who die every year from eating contaminated food are the sad-but-inescapable collateral damage of a food system that must feed more than 300 million Americans every day while meeting their expectations regarding cost and convenience.

Even Marler seemed almost to acknowledge as much. "No one has convinced me that with the population we have, we can go back to a nonindustrial food system. And yet the biggest problem we have is the huge scale of it and the motives behind it. It's a capitalist model, and we've not really figured out how to infuse the system with a good, strong dose of morality."

The issue of morality in the context of our food system is one that fascinates Marler. It informs much of his thinking on the subject of food safety, which often revolves around human nature and how to either counter or encourage it, depending on the circumstances. "We have immediate gratification ingrained in our culture," Marler told me, his face seeming to float in the gray Seattle sky, where a plane was ascending from Seattle–Tacoma International Airport. It bisected his head and disappeared behind a bank of clouds.

Frankly, I was a little stunned by the parallels Marler was drawing between the issue of pathogenic bacteria in our food and systemic arrangements not only in our food system but throughout our society. And by the ways in which these arrangements could be framed in the language of ethics. What Marler seemed to be saying is that the root cause of foodborne illness isn't pathogenic bacteria: It is immorality. It is cutting corners in pursuit of profit. It is viewing someone's kidney failure as a line item in a cost-benefit analysis. It is arguing against more strident testing protocols for fear they'll cut into profits.

Despite his inclination to view pathogenic bacteria in our food as the most visible symptom of a broader malaise, Marler is not a starry-eyed idealist. "It is really hard to get people to understand that our long-term best interests are served by creating food-safety issues that deal with the more structural, systemic problems. But pathogenic outbreaks are something everyone can relate to. Sure, it's only a Band-Aid, but at least it's a Band-Aid that people understand."

Even that may be difficult to apply in a food system that is pulled in disparate and not particularly symbiotic directions: the cost of inputs, highly volatile and entirely beyond the control of producers; the expectations of shareholders, whose motives are primarily financial; and the pressures exerted by retailers and consumers, who want safe food, sure, but not at all costs. Or perhaps any costs. All of which is not to suggest that the producers themselves do not bear responsibility or should not be held accountable; only that the forces and structure of the market and the corporatized nature of the 21st-century food system do not create a fertile environment for addressing the issue of pathogenic bacteria in our food.

Which is why Marler is a firm believer in government intervention. "If we're going to clean things up, it's going to require reengineering the economics of it, and I don't see how you do that without government intervention. The reality is that the only way a society as large and complex as ours is going to work is through government policy."

I began to protest, but Marler raised a hand to interrupt me. "People don't like to hear about government intervention, but they don't seem to mind government intervention that benefits them. It's like all those Tea Party health care protests: 'Keep government out of my Medicare.' The problem isn't government intervention; it's that too often the government intervenes in a way that big businesses like. The job of FSIS is supposed to be ensuring public health; it isn't supposed to be finding a balance between Cargill making an extra 2 cents per pound of hamburger and ensuring public health. But that's what it has become. If those people would just visit the victims, it would totally shift their priorities. The president visits wounded vets; he visits businesses. But no one goes and sits across the table from a 23-year-old kid who ate a hamburger and will never walk again because of it." He paused, as if considering the implications of what might transpire from just such a scenario. "It might make them think, 'You know, maybe I need to up my game a little.'"

At this, I closed my notebook and prepared to take leave. The hour Marler had promised was almost up, and a few minutes prior, an assistant had announced the arrival of his next visitor, an FDA official who, Marler told me, had "something big" to share with him.

But he wasn't quite finished. "I've often wondered what part of the human genetic makeup makes it impossible to put ourselves in other people's positions or to think too far ahead. Because frankly, the way we're heading isn't going to end very well. I mean, what's the world going to look like in 50 years under our current system of incentives?" It was clear to me that he wasn't merely talking about food safety, or even necessarily food at all, but our entire culture, with all its complex, convoluted, and interconnected systems that, at the outset of the 21st century, have begun to reveal their tremendous vulnerabilities. "I think the biggest problem is that we've lost control of our food system."

He leaned back in his chair, just as another plane arced across the steel-colored sky. "It's really hard to imagine sitting back in a half century and saying, 'Wow, this really worked out well, this looks really great.'"

Then he rose and went to talk to the man from the FDA.

5

On a chilly, rain-moist morning in late January, Mark McAfee met me at the door of his home, a sprawling Spanish colonial in the middle of California's San Joaquin Valley. I'd spent the past 3 hours driving southward through the valley, which spans approximately 250 miles on a track that runs from due east of San Francisco to just past Bakersfield, about 90 minutes north of Los Angeles. Much of my drive had been conducted in pre-dawn hours, but for the last 50 miles or so, I'd watched through the periphery of my vision as trees (mostly almond, I later learned) flew by in endless hypnotic rows. Every so often, I'd pass an oasis of neon, where truckers had gathered to sleep off the miles, refuel, and partake of burgers and fries. To my right, a low range of grassy hills paralleled Interstate 5; to my left, just visible beyond the 60-mile-wide sweep of crops, the snow-covered ridges of the Sierra Nevada range slowly emerged from the dark. It was more food being grown in one place than I'd ever seen before, and I spent much of the drive trying to come to terms with the scale and scope of it all.

According to some estimates, California is responsible for as much as 12.8 percent of the United States' agricultural production, and the San Joaquin Valley is where the majority of California's food is produced. It is often called the "salad bowl of America," but in truth, the San Joaquin brings us a lot more than salad. Grapes, strawberries, almonds, raisins, cotton, beef, asparagus, milk, lamb, lettuce: It adds up to an agricultural industry worth $20 billion annually. Almost certainly, at some point in your life—at some point in the past few months or even days, more likely—you've eaten food produced in these fields. The economy of the San Joaquin Valley isn't purely one of agriculture; it is also home to numerous oil wells that tap into California's most productive reservoirs. And prisons. The region is dotted with correctional facilities, including the notorious Corcoran State Prison, the current residence of Charles Manson.

My visit to the San Joaquin Valley coincided with a weeks-long deluge that had forced the evacuation of hillside homes to the immediate east for fear of mudslides and had created shallow pools of water that frequently ran over the road. The water thrummed against the underside of my rental car as I drove. The unplanted fields that unfurled into the horizon were little more than lakes of mud.

An excess of moisture is not typical to the valley; indeed, the San Joaquin's natural condition is one of drought. The region's agricultural economy would likely never have progressed beyond withered subsistence farming were it not for a thousand-square-mile maze of delivery routes that funnel water from the San Joaquin and Sacramento Rivers. These, in turn, are recharged by Sierra snowmelt. One hundred years ago, prior to the New Deal legislation that funded all the canals and dams and levees, the San Joaquin Valley was a seemingly endless expanse of dry, brown, unproductive soil, punctuated by small farming communities that had sprung up around the few sources of natural water. Today, thanks to flows of distant water that course through man-made cuts, it's a 5-million-acre sweep of verdant farmland. "The most productive unnatural environment on Earth" is how historian Kevin Starr referred to the San Joaquin Valley. Although my view was one of lushness and fertility, the flatness and expanse of the valley made it easy to imagine a barren tableau of dirt and dust.

Depending on your view, it's either ironic or entirely appropriate that my quest to understand the roots of food safety had taken me to the San Joaquin Valley, because the valley's role as food producer to the nation is utterly reliant on fragile, human-made systems that now find themselves in the path of a raging battle over the rights to the water that has allowed the region to become so agriculturally productive. As it turns out, creating an oasis of agriculture with an entire populace that depends on the ongoing health of that oasis in a region that's not blessed with much natural rainfall has a downside: water shortages.

For a while, it appeared as if the rivers and canals would never run dry, that there was more than enough water to slake everyone's thirst. But false abundance is almost always the story of natural resources, particularly those whose usual course has been altered by humans. The San Joaquin would prove no different, as drought, population growth, and an increase in demand from the valley's food producers colluded to create acute water shortages at the source points. As if that wasn't complicated enough, an endangered species of fish known as the "delta smelt" began disappearing en masse from its native waters, in part because it was being sucked in great numbers into the enormous pumps that drive the water south. Little surprise, then, that the lawsuits started flying.

The delta smelt may not look like much; the average specimen is about as big as your index finger, silvery in color, and with unfortunately bulbous eyes that appear far too big for its head (all of which is to say, it looks like a fish). It enjoys a 1-year life-span, a dearth of existence that is exacerbated by the fact that it is distinctly bad at reproducing. It is exceptionally susceptible to environmental changes and other disruptions to its life cycle and is considered by biologists to be an indicator of ecosystem health. So as it became increasingly clear that the practice of siphoning water to the San Joaquin Valley was endangering the delta smelt, the water—or, at least, some of the water—that had flowed for nearly a century stopped running. The result was anything but unpredictable: Immediately, the crops began to wither.

There's something else lacking in the San Joaquin Valley, something that profoundly illustrates the incredibly fractured, dysfunctional nature of agricultural production in the United States: food. That's right, the leading food-producing region in the leading food-producing state in our nation is highly food insecure, with over 40 percent of San Joaquin County's adult residents living in a chronic state of uncertainty about the source of their next meal. A 2007 report by the US Census Bureau found that in 2006, six San Joaquin Valley counties were among the 52 poorest counties in the nation.

As I drove through the rainy dawn of a California morning, zooming past what looked to my untrained eye as an endless, if wet, bounty of sustenance, I couldn't help but feel sheepish. I'd come here seeking a more cogent understanding of food safety, and all around me, hidden in the little villages composed almost entirely of Latino farm laborers toiling for meager wages to produce food for people far, far away, there was hunger. It was a stark reminder of just how narrow minded and even presumptuous our definition of safe food has become. Because before you can have safe food, you have to have any food at all.

Mark McAfee pumped my hand energetically and led me into a spotless kitchen that overlooked an inground swimming pool and, beyond that, a herd of grazing cows. He is a tall man, though the breadth of his torso and the beefy fullness of his face make him appear shorter than he actually is. He is by no means fat; rather, he possesses a powerful, top-heavy build I've come to associate with weight lifters (which he is not) and men who've chosen physically arduous careers. For a few minutes, I worried over a nagging sense of resemblance in both face and mannerisms. Then it struck me: Jay Leno.

In simplest terms, I'd sought out McAfee because he founded and runs Organic Pastures (OP), the largest exclusively raw milk dairy in North America. On 550 prime agricultural acres he inherited from his grandparents, McAfee manages a herd of about 400 Jersey and Holstein milk cows (plus 19 bulls for breeding and, at any one time, a few dozen steers for beef). Unlike most modern dairies, where the animals spend their entire lives either inside or in the tight confines of outdoor corrals, OP's bovine residents are given unfettered, year-round access to pasture. The fact that the vast majority of US cows, which are biologically designed to extract nourishment from grass and hay, never set foot on pasture is indicative of the strange, illogical manipulations we've foisted on our food.

Still, access to their natural diet and habitat is by far not the most striking difference between McAfee's operation and the overwhelming majority of North America's dairy industry. No, the most striking difference lurks in that little three-letter modifier, "raw," and it was the real reason I'd made the nearly 4,000-mile journey from my home in Vermont to look at a bunch of cows.

Most (and when I say "most," I don't mean 51 percent; I mean in the neighborhood of 99 percent) milk sold in the United States is pasteurized by heating it to 161°F for 15 to 20 seconds. Some is pasteurized through a process known as ultrahigh-temperature (UHT) processing, whereby the milk is subjected to 275°F for 1 or 2 seconds. Typically, this is accomplished by injecting vats of milk with high-pressure steam; the upshot is that it creates a product that doesn't require refrigeration and has a shelf life of over half a year. UHT is extremely popular in Europe (almost all the milk sold at the retail level in France is UHT processed), but it's been slower to take off in the States, perhaps because consumers are suspect of milk that can be sold unrefrigerated and safely consumed nearly a year after it was packaged.

Raw milk, of course, receives none of this treatment and never reaches temperatures higher than that of the cow's udder, about 101°F. It's impossible to know with certainty what percentage of milk in the American market is sold and consumed raw; owing to widely variant state regulations, a lot of the trade in unpasteurized milk is conducted on the black market. In fact, sales of raw milk are banned outright in 24 states, while eight states allow retail sales. The remainder fall somewhere in between, typically allowing on-farm sales direct to consumers. Some states disallow raw milk sales to humans but allow sales through a "pet consumption" loophole (as if anyone is buying $11-a-gallon milk for Fido). Overall, it is very roughly estimated that 1 to 4 percent of the US population, or 3 million to 12 million people, drink raw milk. That's a big crowd, a lot bigger than I'd ever have guessed, but by any measure it is dwarfed by the number of people who consume pasteurized milk—although it's interesting to note that in rural Europe and Asia, raw milk is still extremely common.

Having been born into and raised in the era of pasteurization, I was rather stunned to learn that it wasn't until after World War II, and the subsequent consolidation of the dairy industry, that the technology came to dominate the market. Oh sure, pasteurization had been around for a while: It was developed by French chemist and microbiologist Louis Pasteur in the mid-1860s as an antidote to the problem of wine and beer going sour (one can only imagine how relieved the masses must have been). But it took a few decades before anyone thought to apply the technique to milk, and another half century or so before pasteurized milk had become the default dairy product available for retail sale in the United States.

To the governmental agencies charged with enforcing the byzantine laws that regulate our food system, mass pasteurization of milk is the greatest food-safety advance in modern times. To advocates of raw milk, it is an ill-conceived if well-meaning blight on the nutritional and food-rights landscape. To understand the former view, one need only consider the dramatic decrease in instances of foodborne illness that followed mass pasteurization. From a pathogenic standpoint, milk has always posed unique challenges, in no small part because it emerges from the underside of a cow, only a few feet from where the animal excretes some 80 pounds of manure each and every day. As someone who was raised and lives in dairy farming communities, I can assure you that a cow's udder is something of a poop magnet.

As such, milk has a long and storied role as a vector of pathogenic bacteria. *Campylobacter jejuni, Listeria monocytogenes, Escherichia coli,* salmonella; milk certainly isn't the only medium for transmission of these nasty little buggers, but prior to pasteurization, it was arguably the most common. That's because milk is a sort of Club Med for bacteria: warm but not too hot, with plenty of protein, fat, and sugars lying around. And you can't wash the bacteria off of milk, as you can with many other foods. Which means that what gets into your milk is almost certain to stay in your milk. And worse yet, multiply.

This helps explain why, prior to 1938, milk-borne pathogens accounted for 25 percent of all foodborne illness (although it's hard to imagine that the measure of foodborne illness was any more exacting 7 decades ago than it is now). Today, that number has dropped to less than 1 percent. Some of this decline can likely be attributed to issues of sanitation and the way cows were kept. Remember, this was before refrigerated transport had risen to ubiquity; for that reason, dairy farms in the 19th and early 20th centuries were often located within city limits, where the cows were typically housed in conditions that could only be described as repugnant. In those days, it was common practice to locate dairy farms next door to distilleries to facilitate the feeding of distillery waste to the unfortunate animals. The result was a quality of milk so compromised that dairy owners often added water, eggs, flour, and pretty much whatever they had on hand to mask the poor flavor. The final product was known as "swill milk."

Still, the cows' diet was only part of the problem. Compound the issue of diet with a few hundred cows standing and lying in a city block's worth of their own piss and shit, and add to that the fact that people had—at best—a rudimentary understanding of how these conditions might contribute to the spread of disease and therefore made—at best—a passing attempt at cleanliness. And because people didn't have mass pasteurization, there was no protective barrier between the fecal matter that inevitably found its way into the milk and the stomachs of those who drank it.

Frankly, moving our farms to the country hasn't provoked much change in the way cows are kept; the modern industrial dairy is not an appealing sight. Often, the cows are parked in crowded, effluent-ridden paddocks, where they bide their time between milkings. The difference is that now we've got pasteurization to cook the bacteria that funnel into our milk.

Still, issues of sanitation aside, there's little question that pasteurization drove down instances of milk-borne illness. Between 1919, when only a third of the milk sold in Massachusetts was pasteurized, and 1939, when the vast majority of it was, outbreaks of milk-borne disease fell by almost 90 percent. Clearly, pasteurization of milk has had a profound effect on public health, although it's not a panacea. In fact, between 1980 and 2005, there were 41 outbreaks and 19,531 illnesses attributed to pasteurized milk and milk products. That's 10.7 times the number of illnesses attributed to raw milk during this period (remember, however, that only 1 to 4 percent of Americans drink raw milk).

Mark McAfee would agree that pasteurization has made a deep and lasting impact on our collective well-being; he just wouldn't agree on precisely what that effect has been. "We're trying to create a sterilized food system, and all we're doing is making ourselves more susceptible to disease. If you want to walk in a rain forest and not get sick, you'd better have a mirror of that rain forest inside. And raw milk can do that." He was pacing about his kitchen, gesticulating for emphasis. The eggs he'd offered me were sizzling and popping in a pool of smoking butter. I kept looking at them hungrily, but he didn't seem to notice. "This idea that we're going to sterilize the world to make everyone safer. . . ." He paused to flip my eggs—yup, burned— and settle on the proper analogy. "It's just a freaking car wreck."

McAfee's contention (a contention shared by most consumers of raw milk) is that pasteurization kills not only the bacteria that can make you sick but also the components that can make you well. These components include immunoglobulins, the antibodies found in the bodily fluids of vertebrates that identify and neutralize foreign objects like bacteria and viruses. And fibronectin, which increases the antimicrobial activity of macrophages, the white blood cells within human tissue. And mucins, proteins that gel and bind to pathogens. The list goes on.

Raw milk proponents assert that the beneficial compounds in unpasteurized milk can mitigate asthma; strengthen the immune system; protect against infections, diarrhea, rickets, tooth decay, and tuberculosis; and possibly even kill pathogenic bacteria in the milk itself.

Here's the rub (oh, yes, there is a rub): There simply aren't a hell of a lot of studies to substantiate these claims. Most prominently and rigorously, the journal *Clinical & Experimental Allergy* published a Swiss study in 2006 that concluded, with a 95 percent confidence interval, that consumption of farm (i.e., "raw") milk "showed a statistically significant inverse association with asthma" and "may offer protection against asthma and allergy." This is the report most often held up by raw milk advocates as proof of the beverage's restorative powers. And for good reason: Most studies on the nutritive powers of raw milk are decades old. In 1937, for instance, the *Lancet* published the findings of a study conducted on two groups of British orphans. Each group comprised 750 boys; one group received pasteurized milk; the other, raw. The group that drank pasteurized milk contracted 14 cases of TB, while the raw milk group suffered only one. "The child on raw milk is very fit," the researchers commented. "Chilblains are practically eliminated. The teeth are less likely to decay. The resistance to tuberculosis and other infections is raised." That sounds nice and all, and perhaps it's simply the choice of words ("Chilblains"? Does anyone get chilblains anymore?), but it seems a quaint version of the rigor we currently expect of these sorts of studies.

One might reasonably wonder why, if raw milk is so obviously beneficial to those who drink it, there isn't a greater body of modern work to support these claims. And why, in a nation that so fervently believes in individual rights, the partial prohibition of raw milk lives on. Depending on whom you ask, the answer to these questions lies in the irrefutable, science-based findings that raw milk is an inherently dangerous product. Or it's based on the fact that raw milk presents an imminent threat to the industrial dairy industry. Or that it might foment a national revolution that will lay waste to the entire corporatized food system. Or that raw milk is such a powerful agent of good health and small-farm vitality (remember, McAfee wholesales his milk at $11 a gallon) that it presents a grave threat to the status quo, which includes the commodity dairy industry, with its $44 billion in annual revenue, and the ever-growing market for the pharmaceutical drugs necessary to treat conditions that could be cured by unpasteurized milk. After all, if raw milk really can alleviate asthma, there'd be little need for the $15 billion annual market for asthma medications.

Although McAfee does not consider himself a conspiracy theorist, his view falls somewhere between the latter two and is shaped in large part by his faith in simple human greed. "When you've spent 100 years designing this battleship called pasteurization, and built huge constructs around that technology, and you've got the ear of the politicians and regulators, of course you're going to protect it." He was scowling a bit, but his face quickly brightened. "But they're on the verge of disaster. All we have to do is pull out 1, 2, maybe 3 percent of the commodity market, and they collapse." He now looked enormously pleased. "We have to reconnect food with medicine. We have to make people understand that raw milk is more than just something to drink. Because when they do, people rejoice."

Well, some people, anyway. There are plenty of folks who do not view raw milk as source of unabashed joy. Or as medicine. Or, if we're to be entirely candid, as a substance that's fit for human consumption in the slightest. These folks include FDA dairy chief John Sheehan. A recluse even by the publicity-phobic standards of most governmental disseminators of regulation, Sheehan is famously on record for likening the consumption of raw milk to "playing Russian roulette with your health." Indeed, the FDA seems to take the raw milk movement very seriously: The agency's Web site includes a 64-page slide show extolling the dangers of raw milk. The conclusion? "Raw milk is inherently dangerous and should not be consumed."

Raw milk proponents—including McAfee—take umbrage at the FDA stance on their favorite beverage. To say that they feel unfairly targeted is an extreme understatement. It's only natural that the largest producer of raw milk in North America would disagree with the FDA's position, and McAfee's ire has been provoked by numerous run-ins with the agency. Most dramatic was a 2007 incident in which the FDA attempted to nail Organic Pastures for shipping raw milk across state lines, a practice that violates federal law. The FDA set up a phone sting, in which an agent posed as a buyer who talked about giving some of the milk to his kids (it was legal at the time for Organic Pastures to ship the milk for pet consumption). The dairy shipped the product anyway, and the FDA had its evidence. Under a plea agreement, Organic Pastures was required to discontinue shipping raw dairy across state lines, whether it was intended for human or pet consumption.

And late in 2006, six California children became infected with *E. coli* 0157:H7; two were hospitalized and one almost died. What did these six children have in common? Why, they'd all either consumed Organic Pastures raw milk or lived in households where the milk was consumed by others, raising the possibility of inadvertent contamination.

Organic Pastures was forced to recall thousands of gallons of its product, and on October 31, 2006, investigators from the California Department of Health Services and the California Department of Food and Agriculture swarmed McAfee's farm in search of the offending bacteria. While they did find *E. coli* 0157:H7 in three cows (McAfee says they were all "dry" cows that were not lactating at the time of the inspection and therefore could not have been the source), the strain of bacteria found didn't match the strain found in the children. Even stranger: It turned out that the sickest of the six children never actually tested positive for *E. coli* 0157:H7, although his primary diagnosis of hemolytic uremic syndrome, a potentially devastating illness that kills about 1-in-20 of its victims, is most often the result of *E. coli* poisoning. The conflicting evidence and lack of a positive test in the HUS victim showcase just how difficult it is to identify, with true scientific certainty, the source of pathogenic bacteria and whether or not it was actually that bacteria that caused the illness. Drawing these connections is often an exercise in probability.

Mark McAfee is not the only raw milk dairyman to feel the FDA's wrath. In 2006, not long after those six children became ill, a Michigan State Police cruiser pulled over a farmer named Richard Hebron near Ann Arbor. The trooper ordered Hebron to step out of his truck and place his hands on the hood; then he was patted down. Hebron's alleged crime? Transporting raw milk intended for human consumption. As Hebron was being held in nearby Lansing, Michigan Department of Agriculture agents and state police officers spent 3 hours rummaging through his home, eventually confiscating business files and a computer. No charges were ever filed.

Whether or not you believe the FDA unfairly targets the producers and distributors of raw milk probably depends on whether or not you view the beverage as a key to well-being or as a potential health wrecker. In my experience from living in a region where raw milk consumption is both legal and prevalent (yes, my family drinks unpasteurized milk, and no, it has not proven to be a cure-all, nor has it ever made us sick), it is one of those foods over which passions run high and reason takes leave. You either believe in raw milk or you don't, and you are prepared to defend those beliefs in the face of all evidence to the contrary. Still, there is at least some noncmotional evidence to suggest that the FDA carries a raw milk grudge. In 2003, a joint USDA/FDA study showed that, on a per-serving basis accounting for the disparity in their consumption, deli meats were 10 times more likely than raw milk to cause illness. Is there a warning against consuming deli meats on the FDA Web site? No, there is not. Is the retail sale of smoked turkey breast banned outright in nearly half the states of our union? Not last time I checked. Has anyone ever been forced to the side of the highway by police officers and had his or her computer confiscated for distribution of baloney? Unlikely.

To McAfee, serving as a regulatory punching bag is simply an occupational hazard and does nothing to dissuade him from spreading the gospel of raw milk. It's clear that he views this as his life's work, and it's clear that he thrives on confrontation. He quotes frequently from *The Art of War* and often frames issues in the language of conflict. "That's our current little battle, and it's a load of fun," he said, after telling me about a fight he was having with the California Milk Pooling Branch over dues he felt were being unfairly levied against his operation. Or, after learning that he was being evicted from Fresno's largest farmers' market because, as he claimed, OP's stand attracted too many customers, "The war is on." Within 3 hours, between fielding my questions, frantic bouts of e-mailing, and frenetic bopping from one end of his operation to the other, he'd identified three possible locations at which to launch a competing market.

Organic Pastures did end up on the wrong end of a lawsuit by two of the *E. coli* victims' families, and rather than have the case go to trial, the company wound up settling for what McAfee deems "a small amount," although I got the impression that McAfee and I might disagree on precisely what constituted "small" in this case. He does not consider the settlement an admission of guilt; nor does he promise that his milk will never carry pathogenic bacteria, never make anyone sick. "I can promise you that my product will make your immune system stronger." We were now in his truck, a mud-splattered Ford with enough stickers promoting his company that the word "raw" appears at least a half-dozen times, and not just on his bumper: The entire truck was an homage to unpasteurized milk. We were driving into Fresno to check on his product at the Whole Foods Market and make a quick stop to see if repairs on his private jet were proceeding apace. (A dairyman who owns a private jet? This was something new. And yes, like his truck, the jet boasts raw milk stickers.) "But I can't promise you it will never make you sick. I just can't."

This seemed like a dangerous admission for a fellow overseeing a $5.5 million annual milk business, and I started to say so, but McAfee was on a roll. "Why do we have poor immunity as a society? That should be a national discussion. The bottom line is that it's everybody's personal responsibility to have a strong immune system, but if you follow the money, it's not in corporate best interests for everybody to take this responsibility. There's no personal responsibility in the equation, and if you don't have personal responsibility, you don't have moral fiber in your country." I was momentarily stunned: Had he just drawn a connection between the consumption of raw milk and the moral fiber of America? Why indeed, he had.

I didn't have much time to consider McAfee's statement, or the ways in which it echoed what I'd heard from Bill Marler, the man who'd led lawsuits against Organic Pastures, because suddenly McAfee spun the steering wheel and we bounced over a curb into a parking lot. My head almost thumped against the side window. "I just had a great idea!" he shouted. "I've got the perfect place for a farmers' market: the old airstrip!" He swerved back onto the street, heading in the opposite direction. "We're going to have the world's first fly-in farmers' market!" He was so enthusiastic that, for a second, I thought it was a great idea, too.

As McAfee pinned the throttle of his truck through downtown Fresno, hell-bent for the airstrip, I thought about how a more complete and holistic definition of "safe food" might read. How it might include issues of nutrition, access, and the right to know exactly where our nourishment comes from, to know what goes into it and how it is produced. Perhaps it should also account for the ramifications of these practices, from soil to seed to supermarket; certainly it should include free and equal access to the research that might condemn or condone them.

And I found myself wondering: Is this the best we can expect of our food? That it not make us acutely ill? Because when you think about, that's a pretty low bar. What about all the people dying long, slow deaths by processed food? What other dangers lurk in our food that aren't accounted for in the CDC's numbers, faulty as they might be?

Because whether or not you believe McAfee's assertions regarding the restorative powers of raw milk, whether or not you feel as if the FDA is unduly harsh in its pursuit of raw milk producers and purveyors, there is clearly a larger story at play. Even Mark McAfee knows perfectly well that most people aren't prepared to eschew pasteurization. "If 100 people walk by my milk in the store, 99 are going to look at it and say, 'Oh, raw milk: That's the stuff that's going to kill me.' But the one is going to buy it because she knows what the benefits are and she knows she can come out here, walk around the farm, shake my hand, see everything we do and how we do it." He chuckled, not at the missed sales or the lost opportunity to spread the raw milk gospel, but at what he views as misappropriated food anxiety.

Maybe I'd simply fallen under the thrall of McAfee's super-charged charisma ("I don't get tired very often," he told me, rather unnecessarily. Then, ever the entrepreneur: "I drink lots of raw milk."), but I could feel my definition of "safe food" taking shape. It is a definition that acknowledges the role of pathogenic bacteria and our evolving understanding of how they spread, and, thus, how to keep them from spreading. "I think about keeping my milk clean all the time," McAfee told me. He conducts his own pathogen testing daily and has almost total control over the processing, bottling, and distribution of his product. While we will never eliminate pathogens in our food, that doesn't mean we shouldn't adhere to basic standards of cleanliness. That doesn't mean that our practices from farm to plate shouldn't seek to limit opportunities for pathogens to catch a free ride.

But at its core, it is a definition based on the largely unspoken truth that widespread outbreaks of pathogenic bacteria are but a symptom of the tremendous distance that has come between our food and us. I mean that both literally—after all, the average piece of food in America travels 1,500 miles to reach your plate—and metaphorically: In an April 2010 response to a lawsuit filed by the Farm-to-Consumer Legal Defense Fund in a US district court for the purpose of overturning the FDA's ban on interstate transport of raw milk, the FDA concluded: "Plaintiffs' assertion of a 'fundamental right to their own bodily and physical health, which includes what food they do and do not choose to consume for themselves and their families' is similarly unavailing because plaintiffs do not have a fundamental right to obtain any food they wish." And

even more plainly: "There is no 'deeply rooted' historical tradition of unfettered access to foods of all kinds."

In other words, you have no right to eat what you want; the
food you can legally access will be tightly controlled by government oversight and regulation. To a certain extent, I'd
always understood this. I knew vaguely how federal agencies
like the FDA and USDA operated and how their duties and
actions often seemed to support industrial-scale agriculture
and food production, with all of its layers of complexity, at the
expense of small-scale, farm-to-consumer trade. But as a citizen of a nation that prides itself on individual rights, that
allows its populace to own and carry concealed firearms,
smoke unfiltered cigarettes, and to speak out openly against
its leaders (all at the same time, if they should choose), I'd
always believed that, fundamentally, I had the right to eat
whatever I damn well pleased. To learn differently was shock-
ing, disappointing, and, frankly, scary. It was as if I'd been
told that I no longer had the right to dress as I pleased or cut
my hair in the style of my choosing. After all, if our rights to
choose the type and source of our food are not "fundamental"
or "deeply rooted," that means we are beholden to the very
system that is responsible for so many recent outbreaks of
foodborne illness and untold incidents of disease caused by
the nutritional deficit inherent to the products of this system.

This was an unsettling train of thought, and I wasn't disappointed when we arrived at the airstrip. McAfee turned off the
street and parked at the edge of the tarmac. Tufts of grass emerged
from cracks in the pavement. It was raining again, and the whole
effect—the gray sky; the empty, dilapidated airstrip; the slow

swish of the windshield wipers—was a little depressing. I had a hard time picturing the place bustling in the way the farmers' markets in my imagination bustle, with vendors under brightly colored tents, selling their wholesome wares to marketgoers swathed in earth-toned natural fibers.

McAfee, it will not surprise you to hear, seemed to have no problem imagining it. "Just look at this place," he enthused. He swiveled in his seat to look out each of the truck's windows, as if the view were so spectacular he didn't want to miss an inch of it. "I'm going to sell so much damn raw milk here!"

6

There's something else besides refrigeration, flush toilets, and corporatized agriculture that was coming to prominence in the early years of the 20th century, and it bears heavily on how we grapple with the issue of pathogenic bacteria. Indeed, if you believe Mark McAfee, it bears heavily on almost every aspect of our well-being. Or lack thereof. To understand what I'm talking about, let's back up to the previous chapter, to the moment I was sitting in McAfee's kitchen, watching him make smoldering ruins out of a perfectly good pair of eggs. *"We're trying to create a sterilized food system, and all we're doing is making ourselves more susceptible to disease. If you want to walk in a rain forest and not get sick, you'd better have a mirror of that rain forest inside. And raw milk can do that."*

Let's forget for a moment that McAfee was speaking in the context of his passion for raw milk; we've been there already. Instead, let's dissect the middle sentence, the one about walking in a rain forest and mirroring that rain forest in your body. This is important and contentious stuff, because it speaks to established scientific assumptions that have given rise to entire industries and defined the manner in which we combat and treat not just food-borne illness but virtually all disease. To understand what I'm talking about, it's crucial to remember that we didn't always know why we got sick. And that according to some people, we still might not fully get it.

Until only a few centuries ago, it was common knowledge that simple organisms could emerge from inanimate objects and that disease was the result of spontaneous generation. When a hunk of decaying meat swarmed with flies, the accepted wisdom held that the meat had given rise to the flies, not that flies had been drawn to the odor and congregated at its source. This theory could be applied to disease, as well: When someone got sick, it wasn't because she'd contracted a germ from some-one else. It was because the conditions in the body were such that disease manifested.

The theory of spontaneous generation was so universally embraced that it became a technique to achieve a desired end. For instance, should one desire a hive of bees, one need only kill a young bull, bury it in an upright position with its horns protrud-ing from the ground, and wait a month. Presto. Bees. (The bees-from-beef theory originated in Greece in about 250 BC.) How elegant and, except for the backbreaking toil of excavating a hand-dug burial hole for a thousand-pound beast, delightfully simple.

It wasn't until the late 1800s that the germ theory of disease took hold, thanks in large part to the efforts of Louis Pasteur (yup, he of pasteurization). Pasteur wasn't the first to propose germ theory; that honor officially belongs to Agostino Bassi, who'd built on the work of a Venetian physician named Girolamo

Fracastoro. In 1546, Fracastoro proposed that epidemic diseases could be transmitted by tiny seedlike particles through direct or indirect contact, and while his work was initially hailed, it soon fell out of fashion. It took another 300 years before Pasteur was able to convince most of Europe that germs were responsible for much suffering, in part through experiments with broth-filled vessels with filtered openings that ensured that nothing could infiltrate. Since nothing grew in the broths unless the vessels were opened, it became clear that the organisms responsible for the contamination came from outside, rather than being spontaneously generated. To understand just how deeply this revolutionized the ways in which we approach health, consider that prior to Pasteur's work, few if any surgeons washed their hands or sterilized instruments between operations.

Over the latter years of the 19th century and the early years of the 20th, germ theory steadily gained prominence, leading both directly and tangentially to the rise of antibiotics, vaccines, sterilization techniques, and those little bottles of antimicrobial hand soap germaphobes carry everywhere. The basic idea is that in order to maintain health, you should avoid germs or, should you become ill, seek out ways to kill the germs that made you sick. Germ theory is why some people wore face masks during the SARS and swine flu outbreaks; it's why we wash our hands before eating and why we tell our kids not to play with money. Germ theory says, in essence, that our bodies are vulnerable to invading bugs, and thus it behooves us to deflect as many of those bugs as possible. No one—not even Mark McAfee—will tell you that germ theory is utterly wrong or that it hasn't saved millions of lives and untold suffering.

What McAfee will tell you, however, is that germ theory isn't merely beneficial; it's dangerous, too. Or, more precisely, that our reaction to germ theory is dangerous. McAfee believes, with a fervor that is itself contagious, that our cultural germaphobia is setting us up for a long, hard fall. "Our bodies are packed with bacteria," McAfee told me shortly after he'd downed a tall glass of raw milk in two long swallows. "We are bacteriosapiens. It's on us; it's in us. It *is* us." To a large extent, recent findings support McAfee's assertion. In June 2008, researchers gathered at the 108th general meeting of the American Society of Microbiology announced that the number of bacteria living within the body of the average healthy adult is estimated to outnumber human cells 10 to one. And furthermore, changes in these microbial communities may be responsible for digestive disorders, skin diseases, and even obesity. This was, in essence, scientific confirmation of McAfee's belief that the bacteria inhabiting us play a role in our response to disease.

It gets even more interesting: Turns out that right around the time Louis Pasteur came to prominence, a fellow by the name of Claude Bernard was exploring a theory that the body's ability to ward off and heal from disease was dependent on its internal environment and general condition. In other words, illness only occurred when the internal environment of the body became favorable to disease.

Bernard died in 1878, but his work was taken up by Antoine Béchamp, a highly learned fellow with degrees in physics, chemistry, and biology. While Pasteur had been promoting the "monomorphic" germ theory (that single-formed, fixed-state microbes are responsible for illness), Béchamp claimed the discovery of tiny microorganisms he called "microzyma." Microzyma were found to be present in all things, whether living or dead, and, according to Béchamp, could take on a number of forms during the host's life cycle. Béchamp believed that the ways in which microzyma evolved were dependent on the chemistry of their environment, or the biological terrain. In other words, and in stark contrast to Pasteur's findings, there is no single cause of disease (the germ). Instead, the biological terrain (i.e., the human body) is populated by microzyma that can morph into something nasty or something entirely benign. Among raw milk devotees, this is known as "terrain theory."

As legend has it, Louis Pasteur would come to believe in the terrain theory in a dramatically last-minute fashion. Supposedly, as he lay on his bed waiting for death to take him (he died from stroke-related complications in 1895), Pasteur called for his assistant and issued something of a confession. "[Claude] Bernard was correct: The microbe is nothing. The terrain is everything." Now, I don't know about you, but to me there is something vaguely suspect regarding the circumstances of this supposed revelation. I mean, we're talking about total capitulation to a theory that refutes pretty much everything to which he'd devoted his entire professional life. On his deathbed. It just seems awfully . . . convenient. It's hard not to wish someone had caught it on video and posted it to YouTube.

Pasteur may or may not have experienced a deathbed epiphany; to me, it doesn't really matter, because it seems perfectly clear that the interior terrain of our bodies has very much to do with how we react to the germs that we encounter every day. Why is it that 100 people can be exposed to the same germ and only some of them will get sick? And why is it that of those who become ill, some get sicker than others? Or have completely different reactions and severity of symptoms? No medical professional dismisses the importance of a robust immune system; that in and of itself is more than a passing acknowledgement that it's not merely the germs you encounter but how your body reacts to those germs. From there, it's not much of a leap to wonder if the foods we eat have an impact—positive or negative—on our immune system. Or, if you like, our terrain.

Still, despite what seems to me like convincing common-sense evidence that the environment inside our bodies has much to do with the degree to which we are affected by things outside our bodies, I couldn't help but feel as if terrain theory contained elements of cultist quackery. Part of this, I'm certain, is that I was raised in the age of antibiotics, in the heyday of germ theory, at a time when antimicrobial hand soaps proliferate and public anxiety over the next killer flu outbreak runs as high as a bad fever. But another part of it is the inescapable truth that Mark McAfee—who introduced me to the theory and so passionately articulated its critical importance not merely in our individual health but in our national health and the proper setting of our moral compass—himself had a certain cultist quality to him. His energy and passion; his unrelenting promotion of himself, his business, and the product of his business; along with his unapologetic, unwavering faith in the restorative powers of raw milk, impart a sort of fervor I've come to associate with fanatical religious figures.

This is not to say I'd been immune to his charisma or unsympathetic to his message. In fact, it was the opposite: Much of what McAfee told me had made perfect, wonderful sense, so much so that it set me on the path to the germ theory/terrain theory debate. But even as I turned down that road, I couldn't help but feel as if I were buying into one of those marginalized wellness theories that proliferate on the Internet. This made me feel slightly embarrassed and hesitant to discuss terrain theory with anyone I thought might not agree with it, as if I were telling them about my experience with alien abductors.

But then something unexpected happened: On March 4, 2010, the science journal *Nature* published a study that essentially confirmed what McAfee was telling me and, by extension, validated Claude Bernard's theory that our internal terrain is key to our health and well-being. The goal of the study was to establish a reference set for the human gut microbiome, and as such, it is written in the sort of impenetrable quasi-language that typifies scientific writing, as if the only people interested in the subject are fellow scientists with the ability to decipher incredibly long sentences built around words that seem to have been constructed with the sole purpose of confusing the hell out of the general population. Actually, it may well be true that these are the only people interested in reading such a study, with perhaps myself as the sole exception.

Still, one quote from the press release accompanying the study's publishing struck me: "Knowing which combination of genes is necessary for the right balance of microbes to thrive within our gut may allow us to use stool samples, which are non-invasive, as a measure of health. One day, we may even be able to treat certain health problems simply by eating a yoghurt with the right bacteria in it." Here it was again: support for the theory that the bacteria in our gut have much to do with our overall health and well-being.

The next month, *Nature* published an article on the subject of human gut microbiology called "Genetic Potluck," authored by Justin Sonnenburg, assistant professor of microbiology and immunology at Stanford University. In the article, Sonnenburg asserted that how we eat affects the microbiota (*microbiota* is the word for a community of living organisms within a particular region) of our guts, both in the short and long terms, and that—here's where I got *really* intrigued—consumption of processed foods can have deleterious effects on our intestinal flora. Sonnenburg wrote: *"Consumption of hyper-hygienic, mass-produced, highly processed and calorie-dense foods is testing how rapidly the microbiota of individuals in industrialized countries can adapt while being deprived of the environmental reservoirs of microbial genes that allow adaptation by lateral transfer."*

To deconstruct Sonnenburg's claim, you need to know about lateral transfer, which is also known as lateral gene transfer (LGT) or horizontal gene transfer (HGT). Basically, LGT is how organisms share genetic material without actually being related. This is in contrast to vertical gene transfer, which is what happens when an organism receives genetic material from its ancestor. Awareness of LGT is a relatively new phenomenon, having first been described in Japan in the 1950s in relation to the transfer of antibiotic resistance between different species of bacteria.

Now that we understand lateral gene transfer, we can understand that what Sonnenburg was saying in his *Nature* article is
the modern industrial diet is depriving our bodies of certain
microbes. The question, of course, is does that really matter? Is
our health affected—positively or negatively—by eating foods
lacking in microbial diversity? I knew Mark McAfee's thoughts
on the subject. And sure, McAfee's a smart enough guy, but he's
no Stanford professor.

So I gave Sonnenburg a call in his office at Stanford, where,
for the past few years, he has been studying the intestinal microbiota and the interplay of pathogens within it—a field of study,
he told me, that has "blown up" in recent years. In other words,
he has personally been conducting and overseeing the sort of
science-based research that could either confirm or deny
McAfee's assertion that good gut health is essential to our ability to ward off disease. To put it bluntly, I called him hoping he
could dequack terrain theory.

I was not disappointed. "There is a lot of evidence to support
the idea that we are a victim of hyperhygenitization," Sonnenburg told me. My ears perked up. "The evidence is increasingly
strong that when our intestinal microbiota is in a normal,
healthy state, we're more resistant to disease. In fact,"—and
here he paused for effect—"one of the top predictors for salmonella poisoning is antibiotic use within the past 30 days." In
other words, when we disrupt the microbial balance in our guts
with antibiotics, or reduce its diversity through sterilization of
our food and environment, we are making ourselves more susceptible to the pathogenic bacteria that inevitably find a way
into our food. If Sonnenburg is right, any attempt to scrub our

food system of bacteria via sterilization, irradiation, pasteurization, or simply cooking the bejeezus out of suspect foods (which these days is pretty much everything) will only further reduce our collective intake of microbes, which will, in turn, only make us more vulnerable. It's like one of those cartoon treadmills that keeps going faster and faster and faster. Except there's no "off" button.

Sonnenburg wasn't familiar with terrain theory (and boy oh boy, did I enjoy giving this particular little history lesson to a Stanford professor), nor was he aware of the debate over raw milk. But, he said, it was "entirely plausible" that consuming foods rich in microbial diversity could colonize the intestine with a degree of microbial complexity that would lead to an overall high level of general well-being as well as—and here's the kicker—providing protection from pathogenic bacteria.

There are some people within the biological science community who are even more certain that the conventional wisdom regarding pathogenic bacteria is, to put it bluntly, killing us. One of those people is Lynn Margulis, a distinguished university professor in the department of geosciences at the University of Massachusetts.

"This whole idea of good bacteria versus bad bacteria isn't just wrong, it's suicidal," Margulis told me. As Margulis explains it, microbes and the communities they produce (which is to say, us) are constantly evolving. When we meddle with that process, we run the risk of unintended consequences that might take hundreds of years to play out. "Some of the things that we now consider pathogens could be key to our survival in the future. I'm not denying there are toxic bacteria, but there are natural reasons for it. When we think of these bacteria as something to be defeated, we are not thinking ecologically at all. The war on pathogenic bacteria is built on lie upon lie upon lie."

Essentially, what McAfee, Sonnenburg, and Margulis are telling us is that sterilized food is safe only in the short term; over the long haul, it degrades our ability to weather incoming invaders and may well have deleterious effects on our overall well-being. Antibiotics provide a convenient analogy: In the short run, they are tremendously beneficial—nothing short of lifesaving—but after only a few decades of widespread use, we are beginning to recognize significant downsides. One is the possibility of secondary infections that take root in the aftermath of antibiotic use; this is because the drugs have knocked out good bacteria along with bad, and good bacteria are, at least in part, what protects us from bad bacteria. The second downside, of course, is that some bacteria have evolved to the point where antibiotics can no longer kill them.

The very real possibility is that sterilized food acts in much the same way. No, it probably doesn't actively kill beneficial bacteria in our guts, but it does subtly, over time, shift the balance of microbes in our system, both by reducing the diversity of the population and by eliminating opportunities for LGT. This situation is exacerbated by the fact that fewer and fewer of us live in close contact with the natural world, where these bacteria proliferate; this eliminates yet another opportunity to be exposed to these microbes. Numerous studies have shown

that children raised on farms have significantly lower incidence of asthma and other chronic conditions associated with
immune response. And when I say "significant," I mean *significant*: One Austrian study found that the prevalence of
asthma was almost 75 percent lower in farm kids. Simply put,
humans are no longer exposed to as much or as varied bacteria
as they once were, and the net effect may well be a society
more vulnerable than ever to the sort of disease that can insert
itself into a bad batch of hamburger and then quietly but
quickly spread across the country.

It should be said that none of this is irrefutable proof that
attempts to expunge pathogenic bacteria from our food—which
will certainly also expunge beneficial bacteria—will only make
us less able to fend off the sort of bacteria that can make us sick
or even dead. To suggest otherwise would be to connect dots
that haven't yet been connected, at least not with the sort of
hard scientific evidence that would compel the scientific community to throw its significant weight behind the theory. But it
would be equally inaccurate to suggest that the more we learn
about the interplay between bacteria, and how the food we consume affects the microbiota of our gut, the more it looks as if
those dots will someday soon be connected.

"One of the things we tend to forget," said Sonnenburg,
toward the end of our conversation, "is that we coevolved with
all these microbes, good and bad. Our ancestors almost certainly ate a far greater diversity of microbes than we do today.
For instance, they used fermentation as a preservation
method, and fermented foods are extremely microbially

diverse. How many people ferment foods anymore?" It was a rhetorical question, so I didn't say anything, but I knew the right answer: not many at all. Sonnenburg continued. "Sterilization and pasteurization of our food have undoubtedly been beneficial to humans over the short term, but there has been a long-term cost, and that cost is exposure to microbes."

Somewhere, Mark McAfee was smugly pouring himself yet another glass of raw milk. And Antoine Béchamp was grinning in his grave.

7

There is another way in which lateral gene transfer relates to the issue of food safety, although in this case, it has nothing to do with the food we actually consume. Instead, it is connected to the ways in which we raise our food.

I will preface this by mentioning that in 2008, a member of my extended family contracted drug-resistant *Staphylococcus aureus,* aka MRSA. This was an alarming but not particularly unique occurrence; a 2007 report by the Association for Professionals in Infection Control and Epidemiology found that these infections were 8.6 times more prevalent than had previously been thought, and that antibiotic-resistant bacteria are found in all wards throughout the majority of US hospitals. In other words, if you walk into a hospital in modern-day America, either as a patient or a visitor, you have a very good chance of being exposed to an antibiotic-resistant bacterium that is difficult, if not impossible, to treat. Oh, and has the potential to kill you.

My relative didn't die from MRSA. She was never even acutely sickened by it. Like the other 30 million or so Americans who carry the bug in their nasal passages, she didn't know she'd contracted it and wouldn't have known but for a routine test (because the bacteria have become so common in medical facilities, many do routine screening). Unless it gets into your blood, typically through an open wound, the condition is actually fairly harmless. It might make your nose itch a bit or cause it to feel as if your allergies were acting up, but you can trot around with the bug for the entirety of your natural life and never know it. Still, an estimated 18,000 Americans annually aren't quite so lucky: In these people, the drug-resistant bacteria make their way into the interior of the body, where they can profoundly affect the vital organs, leading to sepsis, toxic shock syndrome, and flesh-eating pneumonia. All of these conditions are pretty much guaranteed to cause severe illness or death.

To understand how MRSA and the legions of other antibiotic-resistant bugs have evolved, we need to understand a bit about the interaction between antibiotics and bacteria. We also need to know that in modern America, most of the antibiotics produced aren't utilized by the health care industry. In fact, nearly three-quarters of the antibiotics distributed in America aren't even used to treat human beings (more on this in a moment).

Like so many of the other technologies that have redefined our food system and helped shape our definition of food safety (pasteurization, refrigeration, molecular biology), and that we largely take for granted, antibiotics are a relatively recent phenomenon. In fact, the word *antibiotic* wasn't even coined until 1942, although the best-known of this new class of drugs, penicillin, had been around since 1928.

I was intrigued to learn that the word *antibiotic* evolved from the term *antibiosis*, which literally means "against life." At first, I found this ironic; after all, antibiotics have saved millions of human lives and relieved untold suffering in less than a century. But then I began to consider how it is that antibiotics save lives: They kill. Put simply, antibiotics are poisons engineered to kill bacteria, including (hopefully) the bacteria making us sick. They do this by interfering, in a variety of ways depending on the class of drug, with the bacterial cell. For instance, penicillins belong to a class of antibiotics called beta-lactams, which interfere with the peptidoglycan cell wall structure of bacteria. Since human cells don't have cell walls or peptidoglycan, they cannot be harmed, at least directly, by beta-lactam drugs. This helps explain why antibiotics don't work on viruses, which are not independent cellular organisms that are "alive" and can be targeted by a particular drug.

In July 1946, just as antibiotics were going mainstream within the human population, the *Journal of Biological Chemistry* published a research paper from the University of Wisconsin that would have a profound impact on how we feed livestock in this country and, ultimately, on the future of disease and our ability to fight it. It would do one other thing, too: dramatically increase profits for the pharmaceutical industry. The defining conclusion in the UW paper was this one: "Sulfasuxidine and streptomycin singly or in combination lead to increased growth responses in chicks receiving our basal diet supplemented with adequate amounts of folic acid." In other words, if you supplemented a chicken's basic diet with the antibiotics sulfasuxidine or streptomycin, it grew faster than if you didn't.

This finding might not have made such an impact if it didn't coincide with the advent of Concentrated Animal Feeding Operations (CAFOs), areas where livestock is raised in extreme density and fed formulated, rationed diets intended to maximize growth while minimizing inputs and, therefore, increasing profits. The first animals to be subjected to the woes of confinement farming were chickens, thanks (or, from the chicken's perspective, no thanks) to the discovery of vitamins in the early 1900s and the subsequent ability to synthesize them. This led to the realization that rather than keep the birds on grass and soil, where essential vitamins and minerals existed naturally, it would be oh so much more convenient to supplement the feed with these nutrients and bring the whole operation indoors. The convenience to consolidate chicken farm operations was simply too tempting to pass up, and in the 1920s, American poultry farmers began raising their chickens in warehouses, feeding them vitamin-fortified grain. And behold: The CAFO was born.

Not long after the University of Wisconsin released its groundbreaking study on supplementing livestock feed with antibiotics, the FDA approved the practice, so long as the dose was "subtherapeutic" (defined as less than 200 grams, or about a half pound per ton of feed). Not surprisingly, livestock producers lobbied passionately for FDA approval and, on being granted that approval, were pleased to find that the benefits outweighed expectations. In fact, larger animals seemed to respond even more favorably than chickens: Pigs gained about 10 percent more on antibiotic-laced feed, and feed efficiency was improved by 5 percent; beef steers needed 4 percent less feed to reach the same weight in the same period of time.

There was another benefit. Livestock that received routine subtherapeutic doses of antibiotics experienced fewer acute illnesses, which led to fewer culls and condemned carcasses. Now that they needn't fear communicable disease, farmers crowded their animals closer and closer together, and soon pork producers joined the chicken industry by bringing their livestock indoors. And just like that, in a span of barely a decade, animals that had been raised outdoors for thousands of years were shuffled into huge, windowless warehouses, where they'd spend the entirety of their short and brutish lives shoulder to shoulder, nose to tail, beak to butt, eating engineered food and generally being forced to exist in ways that are entirely counter to their nature.

Indeed, although the CAFO model of poultry production preceded the routine feeding of subtherapeutic doses of antibiotics, it is widely acknowledged that without this practice of feed additives, commercial confinement livestock production could not have proliferated and would not have become the prevailing model for all species.

We are just now beginning to understand the glaring deficiencies of raising animals in this manner, deficiencies that range from moral to environmental to health. Still, it must have seemed like a no-brainer at the time: Here we had a miracle drug, one that not only cured humans of infections that had recently been tantamount to a death sentence but also seemed to improve livestock health, even as it caused the animals to pack on more meat over a given time span. In an industry that has long operated on razor-thin margins, a 4 percent gain in feed-to-meat conversion must have felt like winning the lotto jackpot.

And that, in short, is what happens to the other 70 to 75 percent of our nation's antibiotics, nearly 27 million pounds' worth annually. It goes into animal feed, to be consumed by critters that are not acutely ill but nonetheless grow better when the bacterial diversity of their digestive tract has been reduced, creating a noncompetitive environment that allows every precious calorie to be absorbed and targeted for a singular purpose: creating flesh.

It doesn't take a cynic to note that the inclusion of antibiotics in animal feed does not exclusively benefit producers. After all, if the annual US market for antibiotics destined for human consumption is $8.5 billion (which it is), and that spectacular figure represents barely one-quarter of the total national demand, well . . . someone's making an awful lot of dough selling antibiotics to livestock feed producers.

This dandy arrangement—happy producers, happy big pharma, unwitting consumers—continued for a few decades until, in the early 1980s, the CDC caught wind of a sharp uptick in cases of drug-resistant salmonella. In 1984, a study in the *New England Journal of Medicine* drew a convincing line between these cases and the subtherapeutic use of antibiotics in livestock. Still, other than a few concerned science and microbiology geeks, no one got too worked up. After all, this was still the golden age of antibiotics, with new classes of drugs being developed and bacterial resistance—when it did arise—generally applying only to one particular antibiotic and not others. So what if a particular drug was no longer effective against a particular strain of bacteria when there were a half-dozen other drugs that could fill in? The public response was muted to nonexistent.

It should be noted that the mechanisms by which these salmonella bacteria were evolving to survive drugs that had previously rendered them harmless were not entirely unknown. Indeed, drug-resistant bacteria had been part of the national health care meme for decades. The first reported US case of methicillin-resistant *Staphylococcus aureus* (MRSA) showed up in 1968, and it's interesting to consider that the only reason *S. aureus* became resistant to methicillin is because it had already become resistant to penicillin, necessitating a switch to another class of antibiotics.

The thing about bacteria is, basically, that they're smart. Beat them over the head with one stick for long enough, and they'll figure out how to avoid getting hit by that particular stick. So you pick up another, and that works for a while, until it doesn't. And so on, until you end up where we're at today, with an epidemic of MRSA that no longer stands for methicillin-resistant *Staphylococcus aureus*, because it has evolved to the point where it can evade almost anything we can throw at it. Which is why MRSA has recently become an acronym for multidrug-resistant *Staphylococcus aureus*. How convenient that both *methicillin* and *multidrug* begin with *M*.

Now, it has long been accepted wisdom that the evolution of drug-resistant bacteria has its roots in overconsumption of antibiotics by humans. Or, perversely, the underconsumption: The reason you're supposed to finish a full course of antibiotics, even if you feel better many days before the pill bottle runs dry, is to ensure that the drug has completely wiped out the population of nasty bugs in your body. Otherwise, the remaining stragglers might have an opportunity to regroup. Only now, having survived

BEN HEWITT

the antibiotic onslaught, they may well be resistant to future treatment by that particular class of drugs. And, because many of their peers were exterminated by the drugs, they enjoy a competitive advantage.

In any event, it is certainly true that human misuse of antibiotics owns plenty of the blame for creating species of bacteria that no longer fear our current arsenal of treatments. But remember: People consume only about one-quarter of the antibiotics in this country. And as it turns out, the critters that consume the other 75 percent might have as much, if not more, to do with the proliferation of drug-resistant bacteria as we do.

As bad as all this sounds, there are some people who believe it's about to get a whole lot worse. Ellen Silbergeld, a professor of environmental health sciences at the Johns Hopkins Bloomberg School of Public Health, is one of them. Silbergeld was a professor of epidemiology at the University of Maryland School of Medicine when, in 1999, she attended a presentation by a candidate for a faculty position at the university. The presentation was on hospital-acquired infections; according to the presenter, some of the drug-resistant infections floating around health care facilities came from food.

This piqued Silbergeld's curiosity. She knew food could be a vector for pathogenic bacteria, but that didn't explain how the bacteria had become drug resistant. But then, like most Americans, she wasn't aware of the practice of feeding antibiotics to livestock. "When I realized antibiotics were being used as a feed additive, I had an immediate strong sense that there wasn't enough known about this."

116

But how could that be? I asked her. After all, this was only a dozen years ago, at a time when numerous studies had correlated antibiotics in livestock feed with drug-resistant bacteria. Given their critical role in public health, surely these studies would have provoked an immediate and strong response, right?

Well, sort of. In 2006 the European Union banned the feeding of antibiotics and related drugs to livestock for the purpose of promoting growth. But in the United States, the practice remains commonplace, and meat producers have done their level best to discredit the connection between stuffing their livestock with 27 million pounds of antibiotics annually and the drug-resistant bacteria that now claim, by some estimates, over 100,000 American lives each year. Silbergeld believes that our collective disinterest is rooted more in the structure of our regulatory landscape rather than simple ignorance. "I think it fell in a zone between food safety and environmental microbiology. I think the general sense was "This is not my job.'"

So she set out to make it hers. "The idea that it would be a major issue seemed pretty clear to me. The challenge was figuring out how to study it." Silbergeld considered where she'd find the greatest concentration of bacteria coupled with the highest level of animal-to-human exposure. She didn't have to look hard: The Maryland poultry industry produces about 300 million broiler chickens annually, ranking it seventh among all US states in poultry production, despite being the 9th-smallest state in the union. Chicken is such a big deal in Maryland that there's even a recipe known as Chicken Maryland (pan-fried with cream gravy, if you're wondering).

Silbergeld began by studying three groups of people who had direct or close contact with large-scale chicken farms. These included laborers who entered the barns to catch and transport the birds, the workers who handled live birds at the processing plant, and nine people who did not directly work in the industry but lived near these facilities. The results were sobering: Of the nine people living in the community, 100 percent had been colonized with *Campylobacter jejuni,* a bacterium that is harmless to chickens but pathogenic in humans and that is the second-leading cause of gastrointestinal distress in the United States. Occasionally, it causes long-term neurological damage and a form of arthritis called Reiter's syndrome. Interestingly, Silbergeld found that the workers who had direct contact with the live birds fared somewhat better: Of the chicken catchers, only 41 percent were colonized with the bacterium, while the line workers had a colonization rate of 63 percent. Still, it was enough to confirm Silbergeld's fears. "It was clear to me that we were dealing with a significant public health risk."

And the more she looked, the clearer it became. Not long after her initial report, she and five co-workers published the first US-based study of poultry workers colonized by resistant microbes. The startling conclusion? Fully half of the surveyed workers played host to *E. coli* that demonstrated resistance to gentamicin, an antibiotic used to treat many types of bacterial infections. Among the general population, the rate of colonization was a mere 3 percent.

As terrifying as these findings were, Silbergeld's most worrying study underscored the potential for these bugs to spread among an unwitting public. She loaded a passenger car with sampling equipment and lurked in a parking lot near an intersection frequented by poultry trucks. Whenever one of the trucks approached the intersection, Silbergeld would pull into its slipstream and tail it. What she could see was the back of the chicken truck, the birds hunched and scared, their feathers being torn out by the wind. What she couldn't see, but what her sampling equipment would later prove present: high levels of enterococci bacteria settling on the interior surfaces of her car.

Now, *Enterococcus* is a relatively benign strain of bacteria; it's known to cause urinary tract infections and very occasionally meningitis in humans. Okay, so maybe "benign" isn't the right word, but the point is, it's not exactly the next *E. coli* O157:H7. But the problem isn't merely the bacterium itself; it's that a quarter of the enterococci that landed in Silbergeld's car during Operation Poultry Truck proved resistant to antibiotics.

Thanks to lateral gene transfer, the issue is more complicated than that because, as it turns out, the same genes that make a relatively harmless strain of bacteria resistant to antibiotics can make other bacteria resistant, too. "The way we need to think about this is not as the resistance of one particular bug," said Silbergeld. "The real story is of the increased pool of resistance genes that's available to the microbial pool." In other words, the danger isn't so much that you will someday be driving down the highway behind a poultry truck and come in contact with drug-resistant enterococci or some other superbug (not that I'd recommend cruising your convertible along the highways leading to poultry facilities). No, the danger is far broader and more sinister than that: As more and more "resistance genes" are released into the population, more opportunities for LGT are unleashed. And some of that transfer will be in resistance genes.

The question is: Would halting the use of subtherapeutic antibiotic supplementation in livestock feed have a profound impact on the drug-resistant gene pool? Funny you should ask, because after Denmark banned the use of antibiotics in livestock feed for the purpose of growth promotion in 1999, the World Health Organization convened an independent panel to review the consequences in terms of both human and animal health. Their finding? *"Extensive data were available that showed the termination of antimicrobial growth promoters in Denmark has dramatically reduced the food animal reservoir of enterococci resistant to these growth promoters, and therefore reduced a reservoir of genetic determinants (resistance genes) that encode antimicrobial resistance to several clinically important antimicrobial agents in humans."*

In other words, when Denmark banned the feeding of antibiotics to livestock, the reservoir of resistance genes declined.

To help me understand the implications of all this, I called James Johnson, the senior associate director of the Infectious Diseases Fellowship Program at the University of Minnesota and an all-around expert on the subject of Really Scary Bacteria That Can Kill You. It was a phone call that, at least in relation to my ability to sleep at night in blissful ignorance of the realities of drug-resistant bacteria, I wish I'd never made.

According to Johnson, there is simply no question that feeding antibiotics to livestock presents a significant human health hazard and that this hazard is killing people. It's impossible to say with exacting certainty how many Americans die every year from drug-resistant bugs, in part because those most susceptible are often suffering from other ailments that might be listed as cause of death, but Johnson puts the number in the high tens of thousands, perhaps even more. Of course, not every one of these deaths can be attributed to animal feed, but Johnson is certain of one thing: "It's a lot."

To understand why he's so sure of this, you need to understand a bit about where many of these bugs prosper. Which, as it turns out, is in the guts of livestock. Because the bacteria live peaceably and asymptomatically in animals, and because the animals are constantly eating low levels of antibiotics, the bacteria slowly become resistant to the drugs. "These are bugs that simply don't live long enough in humans to gain resistance," Johnson explained. "If a human gets campylobacter, he gets sick, and the bacteria are quickly expunged from his body. But a cow or pig can live with campylobacter for its entire life and never get sick. And if the bacteria are constantly exposed to antibiotics . . . ," he trailed off. "Look, it's not like animals have their bugs and we have ours and never the twain shall meet." In other words, the bacteria that build up resistance and become part of the normal flora inside the guts of livestock are the very same bacteria that can infect humans, with no options for treatment by antibiotics.

What's amazing, notes Johnson, is that awareness of the issue of antibiotic misuse among the medical community has reached an almost fever pitch. Indeed, preventive antibiotic use in the United States has largely been curtailed, even in situations where it has been shown to save lives. Why? *Precisely because of fears over creating drug-resistant bacteria.* "We know that we could save lives if we did widespread preventive prescribing of antibiotics to cancer patients, but we don't because of the concern that we'll create a monster. And yet, here's the meat industry feeding them to our food—not to prevent deaths, mind you, but to make animals grow bigger and fatter. It's so egregious, I don't know how they can do it." To put it even more bluntly: As a culture, we have decided to let some people die so we don't create an environment where drug-resistant bacteria can evolve. Concurrent with this decision, we have created an almost ideal breeding ground for those very same bacteria, so that the meat and drug industries might enjoy increased profits. It boggles the mind, really.

Johnson underscored Ellen Silbergeld's point about resistant genes, which by virtue of LGT can hopscotch between bugs pretty much on a whim. In other words, antibiotic resistance isn't a unique function of one particular bacterium; rather, it is essentially a contagious condition that can be shared among different strains and species of bacteria. Even nonpathogenic strains of *E. coli* (to name but one) can carry resistance DNA that, in Johnson's words, are like "soldiers ready to jump out and attack disease-causing bacteria."

If there's a happy ending to this story, it's this: The FDA is starting to pay attention. In June 2010, the FDA released a draft guidance paper that called the use of antibiotics solely for the purpose of boosting production "injudicious" (probably because they couldn't say "really freakin' stupid") and hinted at phased-in limits on antibiotic use in food-producing animals.

Not surprisingly, the meat-producing councils did not respond with unbridled enthusiasm. The National Pork Producers Council issued a position statement stating that existing

FDA regulations "provide adequate safeguards against antibi-otic resistance." And the National Cattlemen's Beef Association responded: "Antimicrobial resistance is a multi-faceted and extremely complex issue that cannot be adequately addressed by solely focusing on the use of these medications in animal agriculture."

None of which does a whit to change Ellen Silbergeld's mind or diminish her sense of urgency.

"I don't know if this is fully appreciated by the lay public, but we are entering the postantibiotic era. We need to recognize that this is a problem now, not tomorrow or next year. Or we're going to be in big trouble."

8

The issue of feeding subtherapeutic doses of antibiotics to American livestock brought to mind a conversation I'd had in the summer of 2009. That summer, I was reporting a feature story on food safety for *Eating Well* magazine; in the process, I interviewed a woman whose 5-year-old daughter had been stricken by *E. coli* O157:H7, the powerfully pathogenic strain of the bacterium that causes the majority of the serious and life-threatening foodborne illness in this country. It was unmistakably a tale of hardship and suffering, made all the more poignant by the sweet-faced innocence of its victim and the fact that the little girl didn't get sick from carelessly eating a half-cooked hamburger or slice of rancid deli meat. Nope, she got sick because she did what pretty much every parent in this country wants his or her kid to do: She ate her spinach. And ended up on dialysis.

But that's not what struck me. No, what struck me, and struck me so deeply that it in no small part provided the framework upon which this book is built, was a comment the mother made near the end of our conversation: "Eating in this country is an act of faith," she said. Then she paused, before clarifying: "Blind faith, actually."

At the time, I considered her comment solely in the context of pathogenic bacteria, but as the days and weeks went on, I began to realize how aptly it applies to nearly every aspect of our food system. As it relates to feeding antibiotics to animals, we have faith that such a widely adopted practice is, if not entirely in our best interests, at the very least not causing acute human suffering. When we stroll into our supermarket of choice, stocked with all the plenty and diversity we've come to expect from our 21st-century food production and delivery system, we have faith that its shelves will be full. We have faith in the producers and processors that filled those shelves, and we have faith in the systems—financial, ecological, regulatory—that support them. Few of us know where our food originates or who controls the various inputs necessary to bring it to our tables. We simply have faith that their interests (read: money) will continue to align with ours (read: getting fed), and that nothing beyond our control will interfere with this mutually beneficial arrangement. And, of course, we have faith that the food stacked in such seductive abundance won't make us sick.

It is the latter faith that has captured our attention of late, and with good reason. But it's important to recognize the ways in which this faith is built on so many others, until they form a sort of rickety ladder of misplaced trust and assumptions that leave us exposed and vulnerable in ways we rarely, if ever, consider.

"Ah," I hear you saying, "but isn't this the way of modern commerce, with its complex supply chains and just-in-time delivery systems?" Well, yes, that is true: Few of us understand or feel the need to examine the minutiae of how an iPod or a car or a pair of jeans was brought forth from raw materials and delivered into our hands. But there is a fundamental difference between your iPod and your food, and it's best summed up this way: One is essential to your survival. The other—no matter how much you value your David Lee Roth–era Van Halen MP3 files—is not.

And yet, I did not grow up thinking about food. Or more precisely, I did not grow up thinking about where my food came from or how it got to my plate or if it was, in any sense of the word, safe. This is good and, I'd argue, exactly as it should be, particularly for a child. Instead, I was free to concern myself with the matters at hand, which revolved primarily around my attempts to get my mitts on the good stuff: cookie dough ice cream, for instance. Maybe some Cool Ranch Doritos. Or a hot dog. With ketchup *and* mustard. Relish, too, come to think of it.

These are not unusual concerns for a young child, but mine were perhaps more poignant, as my mother was unambiguously of the late-1960s back-to-the-land movement. This necessitated (or at least she believed it necessitated) that she frequent the cramped aisles of funky food cooperatives, where the dried beans and flour were sold in bins to be scooped into reusable cloth satchels and the insufferable scent of patchouli hung in the air. There was not a Cool Ranch Dorito to be found, and if there was any ice cream in these joints, it was conspicuously free of cream, having been hewn from the byproduct of crushed soybeans. If ever there were a food product that should be destined for hell, it is soy milk ice cream. Come to think of it, send the tofu hot dogs down there, too.

My mother wasn't a total food misfit; I've never tasted wheatgrass juice and I never intend to. I was allowed the occasional injection of junk food, but I surely had to work harder for it than most. I should point out, particularly to my dear mother, who is sure to read this, that I am deeply grateful my childhood was not fueled by the half-foods I yearned for. Were I given the freedom to choose my dietary path as a youngster, I'd probably be walking around with a bottle of insulin, a syringe, and a mouthful of rotten stumps for teeth.

Yes, I might arguably have been a bit too fixated on feeding my Doritos jones, but in other matters, I did not consider my food. I didn't think about where the co-op got its pinto beans. I didn't think about where those beans were grown, who provided the seed, who owned the land. I didn't think about whether my beloved birthday hot dogs were constructed of the flesh from one pig or 100; I didn't worry that they might make me sick. (Okay, so they almost *always* made me sick, but that was only because I typically ate my age in hot dogs. Hot tip: This trick only works until about your 7th birthday.) In short, I trusted my food with the unshakable faith of someone who'd never even considered that it shouldn't be trusted. And my mother, despite her obvious preference for feeding her family out of health food stores, did the same.

Who can blame her? This was back in the seventies, before it was trendy to consider where our food came from, long before the word *locavore* had been coined and inserted into the public consciousness. It was before the first reported outbreak of *E. coli* O157:H7 had alerted Americans to the acute danger of contaminated food. Heck, even Wendell Berry had hardly touched on the issue of agriculture and its place in the fabric of American life. Whether our collective disinterest in the means of our nourishment could be termed blissful ignorance or willful ignorance hardly matters (though it was probably both). The fact is, few of us really cared. Few of us even knew that we *should* care.

It's amazing, really, to consider how quickly we arrived at this disconnect. It would be convenient if we could ascribe a single cause, if for no other reason than we'd know better how to change things. But it's not that simple. In the half century prior to my birth in 1971, we lived through the rise of urbanization, food corporatism, and the service economy. We saw the automobile and air travel evolve from curiosities to ubiquities. Unnoticed by most, but equally crucial, we ushered in the age of chemical fertilizers, allowing us to temporarily boost the productive capacity of a given piece of land by double-digit percentages. Any one of these factors would have been enough to begin severing the ties to our food. Together, they became a force that simply couldn't be resisted.

If it sounds like we were innocent, unwitting victims to this confluence of events, well, that's partly true. The fact is, most of us weren't paying attention, and the few that were must have felt the frustration of a tree falling in the forest: They could make as much noise as they were able, but nobody seemed to hear.

But it's equally true that the vast majority of us were all too willing to relinquish control of our food, and there's a simple reason for this: Feeding yourself is damn hard work. I'm not talking about nuking a platter of precooked chicken fingers (though lately, even that seems to demand more ambition than most of us can muster). That's not feeding yourself; that's eating. Feeding yourself requires knowledge of seed and soil. It requires blisters and backaches. It requires land, probably less than you think, but still: land. Who has land anymore? Such a thing seems almost quaint. Feeding yourself takes time, and probably more time than you imagine. It is not, at least in a strictly financial sense, remunerative. If it's money you're looking for, you're better off getting a job pumping gas or working at the local burger joint than growing your own lettuce.

It is currently fashionable to rail against the corporate interests that have drawn a curtain between our food and us. I am not suggesting that they don't own much of the blame. Still, it seems to me that we've been awfully quick to exonerate ourselves. The strange constructs of our culture and economy that make it easier and more profitable to write iPhone apps, or sell cars, or manage a hedge fund, or, yes, write books than it is to grow carrots—this is an arrangement we've agreed upon. To exchange the shovel and hoe for a computer and an Internet connection is no small luxury, and even though many of us complain that we work too hard and too long, for not enough pay, we only complain in the context of the briefest of histories. It's been a century or maybe a little more since most Americans knew the reality of producing food. Heck, if you're eating wholesome food, or are simply blessed with the sort of genes that can survive a hundred years' worth of bad eating habits, that's barely a lifetime. It requires only the most cursory examination to reveal that our food and the ways in which it is produced, processed, distributed, and sold have changed more in the past 30 years than in the preceding 200. Our cultural amnesia is remarkable in its breadth and ability to eradicate the majority of our food history. But then, maybe that's because we *want* to forget.

Now, there are all sorts of reasons for this massive and recent shift in the way we eat, but in truth, they all fall under one umbrella: food corporatism. And food corporatism is really only a century-old phenomenon. That's not to say that 100 years ago corporations weren't in the business of food. In fact, the previous 100 years had seen a decline in the percentage of the US population that farmed, from nearly 90 percent in 1800 to 38 percent in 1900. But since then, we've quadrupled the number of stomachs that need filling while we've reduced the number of farmers that fill them from 28 million to a paltry 1.9 million. To understand just what a dramatic adjustment this is, consider this: If 38 percent of our population still worked on farms, we'd have 120 million farmers. Instead, we now have nearly four times as many prisoners in the United States as we do farmers.

Given these seismic shifts, it should come as no surprise that a century ago, the commerce of nourishment was a quaint precursor to the international conglomerates that preside over the modern agricultural and food landscape. It wasn't quite trading cups of sugar over a white picket fence, but it wasn't far off. In 1903, Kraft Foods, now the largest food and beverage company headquartered in the United States, was founded. It was an inauspicious beginning; by the end of the year, the company posted losses of $3,000 and a horse. Today, Kraft sells $42 billion worth of products annually. In 1900, the agricultural products giant Monsanto did not exist; today, it controls, by some estimates, 90 percent of the seed genetics globally. In 1900, Tyson Foods did not exist. Today, it is the second-largest processor and marketer of beef, chicken, and pork in the world. In its Wilkesboro, North Carolina, plant, one of the company's dozens of US poultry processing facilities, Tyson dispatches two million birds each week.

It is not exactly a coincidence that the emergence of food corporatism corresponded with a precipitous drop in our nation's farm population. As food became a business, it became essential that it be produced and distributed according to the tenets of business. Growth. Efficiency of scale. Shareholder returns. Limits to liability. Quantifying the viability of a small farm according to these metrics is not likely to result in the continued existence of that farm, not unless its owner is inclined to make what amounts to a vow of poverty.

Concurrently, shifts in farming technologies and techniques tilted in heavy favor of the farm as corporation. A century ago, the term "horsepower" actually meant "horse power," as in the power output of an actual horse. You know: head, tail, hooves, teeth, poop. Those sorts of things. A draft horse can outwork even the fittest human by a wide margin, but when you start shoving the power output of 50, or 60, or even 160 of them under a hood? Well, that's when "horse power" becomes "horsepower." And, okay, so $42 billion might not seem like as much money as it did a few years ago, but the fact remains: It's still a lot of dough, and you simply don't run a $42 billion company on horse power. Of course, it's not fair to say that machines alone gave rise to food corporatism; the factors are more complex and nuanced. But it *is* fair to say that without modern, mechanized ag equipment, our food system could never have become so industrialized and so concentrated in the boardrooms of a few.

There's another thing that could never have happened: We couldn't have produced so damn much food. We're up to 3,800 calories per person per day, which is about 1,500 more calories per day than any of us needs, particularly given that most of us don't engage in regular physical activity (you know, like farming). This has given rise to a peculiar and extremely recent phenomenon: Our food is chasing us. It's chasing us because there's more food available than can be eaten, and if it doesn't chase us, through marketing and engineered appeals to our instincts, it won't all be eaten. And if it's not being eaten, it's not being sold. In the world of food corporatism, that would be a very unsavory outcome indeed.

There are all sorts of reasons why this won't be the case forever, but for the time being, the fact remains: After 200,000 years of relatively slow, steady evolution since the dawn of agriculture, it took us a mere 100 years to utterly reinvent our food system. In barely more than a generation, we have shifted from a world in which many of us spent our waking hours chasing food, whether literally through the wild or metaphorically through the growing season. Culturally and individually, we understood the connection between weather and soil and food. Between labor and food. Between food and life. Now, most of us just eat. A dwindling few of us even cook.

If it is easy to forget just how new this arrangement truly is, it is probably because we have no context for remembering an alternative. Everyone reading this book was born into the emergence of food corporatism, and not into its early, fumbling beginnings, when a company like Kraft still sold only cheese and could post losses of three grand and a horse. No, we were born right into the sweet and salty center of it all, the golden age of food marketing, where what you eat is what you are, and not in the naively quaint way your grandmother believed, but in a way that defines your station in life. Eat this, be that. Eat that, be this. And seduced by the slickness and wit, by the salt and sugar and fat, we ate it up.

It's not merely the fare itself that makes up this new food order, because food does not simply happen (despite continued ardent attempts to make it so). The ever-increasing use of laboratory-derived synthetic fillers and flavors that find their way into every aisle of the modern supermarket cannot disguise the fact that, no matter how adulterated, all of these products have their beginnings in raw ingredients that grow in actual dirt. Corn, soybeans, wheat; for all our expertise at chemically tweaking food to maximize its appeal and shelf life, the building blocks of our nourishment are still rooted in the land. This could be seen as encouraging; after all, isn't it nice to know that at least in some distant way, your food is connected to nature?

But it is also worrisome, because the same trends that have reshaped the business of growing and producing food over the past 100 years are now reshaping the elemental building blocks of that business. In a world where population trends seem impervious to resource limitations, ownership of literally millions of acres of farmland is being transferred to corporations, hedge funds, and nation-states every year. What do these investors see that others don't? Several things, actually. They see the rapid disappearance of farmland, at a global rate of nearly 20 million acres per year. They see the pace of population growth, and they wonder how we'll feed 50 percent more mouths in 2050. They see impoverished African and Eastern Asian countries, still reeling from the worldwide recession, eager to sell prime agricultural land for pennies on the dollar. Then they extrapolate from these factors, and they realize that we are in the midst of a high-stakes, real-life game of global monopoly. Like oil, farmland is a nonrenewable resource. Unlike oil, life without it isn't merely inconvenient: It's over. So they go all in, betting that farmland will be the next Park Place. In Ethiopia, where more than 13 million people need food aid daily, the government is offering more than 7 million acres of its best farmland to the highest bidders. In total, more than 100 million acres of African farmland has been—or is in the process of being—acquired by both private investors and governments. All of this has happened in only the past few years.

If this seems rather disheartening, make no mistake: There has been, of late, a food awakening. We are on the cusp of a new era in how we feed ourselves. For the past half century or so, the options have been, to put it mildly, limited. But largely for reasons of health, and spurred on by folks like Michael Pollan, author of *The Omnivore's Dilemma,* and Eric Schlosser, author of *Fast Food Nation,* we've started asking questions. *What's in this? Where did it come from? Why are there so many ingredients? And why can't I pronounce half of them?* The pushback against the industrial food system was so sudden and so energetic, it's easy to forget that Pollan's hugely influential book was published only a handful of years ago.

The result has been a remarkable expansion of food choice in remarkably short order. Depending on where you live, where you shop, and your personal inclinations, you've got your industrial conventional, your industrial organic, your localized conventional, and your localized organic. You can buy from a supermarket, from the organic section in said supermarket, from a Whole Foods Market, from an independent health food store, from a food cooperative, from a farmers' market, and even from the farmer herself. Like an increasing number of Americans (43 million, give or take a few), you can grow a garden or, if you lack the ground space, keep a few containers on your windowsill. This is very good news, especially for those of us who can afford to be selective about where our dinner comes from.

But across the full spectrum of those choices, there are pitifully few who don't play by the rules of food corporatism. And to believe that individually any one of us is immune to the hazards of those rules just because we eat all organic, or because we're on a 100-mile locavore diet, or because we grow really nice arugula in the backyard is to engage in self-delusion. The world is too big; there are too many mouths to feed. We need food, and lots of it, and the risks that run throughout the tangled web of our food system are too pervasive for any of us to hide from them. We simply do not have the infrastructure in place to peacefully absorb the dismantling of industrial food and all the threats it contains.

Which means that our food system isn't just big. It's bigger than us.

9

Our culture has become almost completely severed from the sources of its nourishment. Everywhere I looked (and I didn't have to look hard), I found examples that illustrate this disconnect: in the meat industry, where a mere four companies control 80 percent of the processing market, a sharp uptick from 3 decades ago, when five companies owned only 25 percent of the business. Or in the dairy industry, where between 1970 and 2006, the total number of farms in the United States fell almost 90 percent from 648,000 to 75,000 even as milk production doubled. Examples can even be found in the organic foods industry. In 1995, there were 81 independent national organic brands. By 2007, all but 15 of these had been absorbed by multinational food processors. I was a little shocked to realize that these changes have happened roughly in my lifetime.

But these examples pale in comparison to the one industry that underpins all of our food, an industry in which increasing consolidation, scale, and control have become so pervasive that the US Department of Justice recently launched an antitrust probe into the practices of its dominant player. It is an industry that operates largely outside the boundaries of public awareness, in no small part because, unlike food, the products it trades in are not part of everyday American life; yet, conversely, they are utterly critical to the food supply chain and therefore to life itself.

If I didn't need to look hard to find my previous examples of consolidation and control, I *really* didn't need to look hard to find this one. I needed only to descend a flight of stairs to the dark confines of our basement, where my wife, Penny, keeps a cardboard box full of seed packets, the remnants of the spring's garden planting.

If you're like most Americans, it's been an awfully long time since you thought about seeds. This is understandable; the packaged food that dominates modern supermarkets gives few hints as to its true origins, as if it simply emerged from the bowels of a factory somewhere, a sort of Immaculate Conception of calories. Actually, this is partially true: Most modern processed food did emerge from a factory, and increasingly, the components of 21st-century food—the flavorings, the preservatives, the coloring—are the stuff of laboratory science rather than nature. But at one point, a point far down the supply chain from most of our dinner tables, the raw building-block ingredients for that processed food emerged not from a factory but from the soil. And this most definitely did not happen by Immaculate Conception: It happened because somebody planted a seed.

Given seeds' crucial role in supporting humanity, it is stunning how quickly and completely we've managed to sever our grasp of the connection between food and seed. It might sound

patronizingly obvious to mention this, but I believe this disconnect has become so complete and pervasive that mentioning it
is justifiable: Seed begets all food, either directly (fruits, grains,
and vegetables) or indirectly (meat and dairy animals that are
fed on grain and grass). In the modern food economy, there is
something almost quaint in the notion of planting a seed, as if it
were some sort of ancestral ritual that went out of style with our
great-grandparents.

Of course, seeds don't just control and determine our food.
This morning, like every morning, I rose from a bed clad in cotton sheets to dress in clothing sewn from cotton. Did I consider
even for a moment that cotton is a crop and, like all crops, the
result of seed? Frankly, I did not. And how many of us pause
before we refill our prescription at the corner pharmacy to give
thanks to the seed that grew the plants that were engineered
into the drug that alleviates our symptoms? Not very many.
These are rhetorical questions, because you know the answers
as well as I do. We seem to understand that agriculture is the
foundation of modern society (though even this connection can
feel tenuous), but for some reason—perhaps because it simply
doesn't occur to us, perhaps because few of us have anything to
do with agriculture these days—we fail to follow this line of
thought to its obvious conclusion: Without seed, there is no
agriculture.

It would be unwise to assume that nobody's making these connections; it would be equally unwise to assume they're making
these connections for strictly altruistic reasons. The global seed
trade is a fruitful one, worth nearly $43 billion annually. In the
21st century, this sweet and juicy pie is split (not very amicably, it

should be noted) primarily by a handful of international conglomerates. In agricultural circles, they're known as the "Gene
Giants" because, as you'll see, the industry of seed is really an
industry of genetics. It is an industry of chemistry and science
and the ruthless pursuit of market share. Monsanto is leading
that pursuit by an astonishing margin; the company now controls
about a quarter of the global seed market, while its closest competitor, DuPont, clocks in with about 15 percent. All told, the top
three seed companies—Monsanto, DuPont, and Syngenta—own
approximately half the market.

But that's only part of the story, and to understand why, you
need to understand the ways in which we've manipulated seeds
to do our agricultural bidding. This has happened since the
dawn of agriculture, but only began in earnest in the early 1900s
as plant breeders sought ways to develop and strengthen particular traits. For instance, maybe you (I'm talking about the 1910
version of you, with your little farm in the country and stable full
of draft horses) grew a variety of corn that was particularly sweet
but slow to mature. And maybe you grew another variety of corn
that didn't taste so hot but ripened to maturity much more
quickly. And let's say you got sick of choosing between really
yummy corn that wasn't quite ripe and really ripe corn that
wasn't quite yummy. What to do? Why, being the crafty farmer
you were, you determined that if you stripped the tassel from the
plants whose traits you wished to suppress, the offspring of the
tasseled and de-tasseled plants would be a step toward a variety
that was both yummy and rapidly maturing. It might take a few
seasons of this sort of orchestrated plant sex to achieve the
desired results, but that was okay: I mean, we're talking about

the early 1900s. You didn't have a television and a Twitter account. You had time to mess around with this sort of stuff.

It's impossible to overstate the impact of hybridization on the then-nascent commercial seed industry and on agriculture in general. In part this was because hybridization held massive potential to improve yields, flavor, and climate and soil suitability; basically, everything that makes a crop desirable. Indeed, hybridization of seed is one of the primary contributing factors to the stunning rise in agricultural yields over the past half century or so. Hybrid varieties of corn became widely available in the mid-1930s; it's no coincidence that over the 2 decades that followed, corn yields doubled. Some of the increase was due to evolving technique and equipment technology, but hybridization was undoubtedly the root cause.

Still, there's another aspect of hybrid seed that's equally if not more crucial to the development of an industrial seed complex: Since the seed from the first generation of hybrid plants does not reliably produce true copies, saving hybrid seeds from year to year is a gamble; the traits that will carry forward from each of the original varieties cannot be predicted. This is sort of fun if you're a home gardener but decidedly less so if your livelihood depends on consistent production of quality crops. In other words, if growers want to realize the full benefits of a hybridized plant, they are by default forced to purchase new seed each and every year. This reliance on hybridized seed has led to a virtual halt on development of non-hybrid varieties, at least among the major industry players, who value hybridization not just for increased yields, but for the fact that it pretty much guarantees repeat business on an annual level.

These days, purchasing fresh seed is accepted as the norm; very, very few people, whether they're full-time farmers or casual gardeners, save the seed of crops from year to year (seed saving is not terribly difficult, but it is time intensive). But much as it is a relatively recent phenomenon to walk into a supermarket and walk out with a carton of heat 'n' eat chicken parts, the notion that a vegetable grower can simply order his or her seeds of choice every year is not backed by a lengthy history. As recently as about 80 years ago, there wasn't much of a private seed industry in the United States, or anywhere else for that matter. Up to this point, seeds were obtained through farmer and gardener exchanges, via on-farm seed saving, and through the handful of mail-order companies that existed at the time.

There was one other large-scale seed supplier: the US government. Our nation's leaders were motivated by a simple objective: to generate the food security that would fuel the growth of a nation in the 19th century. Delivering seeds to the citizenry furthered this cause in two ways. Most obviously, it provided the raw materials necessary to produce food. Less obviously, but over the long haul no less important, it created a nation of citizen plant scientists who, through the necessary labor of growing food and saving seed, helped evolve the genetic makeup of staple crops to perform in a variety of ecosystems.

This was necessary because so few of the foods we've come to rely on are native to North America. Sure, the United States in the early 1800s was already an agricultural society, but it was sorely lacking in plant diversity and vitality. Of the world's 40 most prominent food and industrial crops, North America has contributed only one: sunflowers. Besides the sunflower, the only crops indigenous to North America are the blueberry, cranberry, Jerusalem artichoke, and pecan. What, no corn, you ask? That's right: Corn (or maize, as it was known to the Native Americans and early settlers) was developed from a wild grass that originally came from what is now southern Mexico, some 7,000 years ago.

No wonder those early settlers were so damn skinny; no wonder that in the early- and mid-1800s, the collecting of seed was considered so important to American interests that the navy regularly sent ships on plant expeditions. They returned with a tremendous diversity of cultivatable goodies in their holds, including such staple crops as beans, rice, cotton, and wheat.

As this genetic plant material arrived on the shores of our young country, the US Patent and Trademark Office (PTO) and congressional representatives oversaw the propagation and distribution of billions of seeds throughout the US territories. The program was a huge success. By 1861, some 2.4 million bundles of seed, each containing five packets, were distributed. In 1897, the initiative reached its zenith, with the mass distribution of 1.1 billion packets. By this point, the USDA was running the program, which accounted for 10 percent of the agency's annual budget.

I find it stunning to consider that barely more than 100 years ago, the US government so actively facilitated its citizens' efforts to grow their own food. How new our country truly is; how incredibly quickly things have changed.

This munificence would not go unnoticed. We are, after all, a capitalist nation, and it did not take long for entrepreneurial minds to consider the squandered profits inherent to the government's seed program. The earliest tangible evidence of that attention came in 1883, with the formation of the American Seed Trade Association (ASTA), which immediately applied itself to lobbying for the demise of the congressional seed program. Still, the seed program enjoyed strong populist support (something for nothing, and all), and it took more than 4 decades of intense pressure by ASTA to convince the USDA to slash it. Whether it was intentional or not, the foundation had been laid for a private, corporatized seed industry, though it's probably safe to assume that no one imagined just how private and corporatized it would become.

For another few decades, the business of seed remained the business of regional companies serving regional economies. There was a heady rush of progress in hybridization, as private money and the research it funded swept through the industry, but the localized nature of the business and the widely variant needs of its consumer base, from victory gardener to monocropping pioneers, ensured a high diversity of offerings. (Monocropping is the practice of sowing the same crop in the same soil, year after year after year. It offers a high degree of short-term economic efficiency, but because different plants deplete the soil of different nutrients, it requires massive applications of fertilizer and chemicals.)

Despite a handful of seed company buyouts throughout the 1960s and 1970s, it wasn't until the 1980s that industry consolidation began in earnest. Suddenly, companies that had previously shown little to no interest in the business of seed were throwing hundreds of millions of dollars into the ring. In only a few years, mergers and acquisitions utterly reshaped what had previously been a relatively quiet cottage industry, albeit one that served a critical role in the continued survival of our nation.

This rapid shift had its roots in a most unlikely place: a research laboratory at General Electric, where a genetic engineer named Ananda Mohan Chakrabarty had developed a bacterium capable of breaking down crude oil. Chakrabarty immediately recognized the potential of his discovery in the treatment of oil spills (and his employer, no doubt, recognized the financial rewards that would accompany such a technology) and quickly filed for a patent. But Chakrabarty had a problem: His invention was, strictly speaking, a living thing. And US law dictated that living things could not be patented. A legal scuffle quickly erupted, and on June 16, 1980, the US Supreme Court ruled in Chakrabarty's favor.

What does any of this have to do with seeds? Plenty, as it turns out, because the ruling paved the way for the patenting of life based on its genetic coding. In other words, the specific genetics of a seed—the functions that make it able to create a certain crop with certain characteristics—could now be protected by patent. If you developed a soybean seed that improved yields by, say, 12 percent on a given acreage, that seed was yours. For as long as your patent was active, no one else could produce a soybean seed with the same genetic makeup without your express permission. Would you be willing to lend that permission? Why, sure, of course you would: for a price.

The response was massive and nearly instantaneous. With essentially zero regulatory oversight, an entire industry was transformed virtually overnight. What had previously been a public resource—the genetic structure at the heart of everything we put on our plates—was transferred to private hands in a matter of months. And to whom was this wealth of information conveyed? Mostly to chemical and pharmaceutical companies. At first blush, this might not seem a likely bunch to be dabbling in agriculture. But for two reasons, they were a perfect fit. For one, they had the dough. Still, lots of companies from lots of industries had money, so there must have been something else. And that something else was their ability to see inside the seed to the genetic material within. To a chemical or pharmaceutical company, a seed is merely a congregation of genetic material that can be tweaked, bent, and otherwise modified to achieve a particular outcome. And suddenly, those genetics were patentable. Party time.

The Chakrabarty ruling wasn't the only piece of legal framework that paved the way for massive privatization of seed genetics. Coincidentally, even as the US Supreme Court was considering Chakrabarty's case, US Senators Birch Bayh (D-Indiana) and Bob Dole (R-Kansas) sponsored a seemingly inconsequential piece of legislation known as the Patent and Trademark Law Amendments Act of 1980. The Bayh-Dole Act, as it would come to be known, provided the legal means for transfer of university-generated, federally funded inventions to the commercial market. In other words, and as it relates to the business of seed, public universities engaged in biotechnology research (as many were and are) could now sell the results of this research to the highest bidder. At which point the highest bidder could then commercialize the technology and sell it back to the very public that, through taxes and tuition, had funded its conception. Neat trick, eh?

And so it is no coincidence that in Monsanto's company timeline, the entry next to the year 1981 reads: "A molecular biology group has been set up and biotechnology is firmly established as Monsanto's strategic research focus." It is no coincidence that prior to 1980, Monsanto did essentially no seed business. It is no coincidence that now it sells nearly twice as many seeds as its nearest competitor.

As alarming as it might seem that only three companies account for half the global seed market, this fact is not fully indicative of how lopsided the market has become. By some estimates (not Monsanto's, it should be noted), Monsanto's patented genes are currently being inserted into roughly 95 percent of all soybeans and 80 percent of all corn grown in the United States. By way of complex and highly confidential licensing agreements with other seed companies, Monsanto's reach extends far beyond its own products. "Monsanto has been very aggressive. I think they're following a strategy of control," Neil Harl told me, when I called him at his vacation house in Hawaii. Harl is a professor in agriculture and an emeritus professor of economics at Iowa State University. I'd tracked him down because he's somewhat unique among the growing tribe of Monsanto-bashers in that he holds no particular disdain for industrial agriculture. But even in the corporatized world of modern food and agriculture, Harl believes that Monsanto has been allowed to amass too much influence. "When you have high levels of concentration, ultimately the holder of that power is going to use it to their benefit. The level of control is unbelievable."

It's worth repeating a point I made earlier in this chapter, though perhaps not emphatically enough: *Nothing is more critical to human survival than seed.* If, like most people, you've never thought much about seed, you might need a moment or two for this to register. That's okay; it took some time for me, too. But my statement is nonetheless true. Seed provides the food we eat and the clothing we wear. Without seed, there could be no agriculture; without agriculture, humans would still be scouring the forests for nuts and berries and bludgeoning the occasional beast with a throwing stick. In other words, without seed, life as we know it would not exist. Indeed, most of *us* would not exist. It has been said that whoever controls the money supply controls the people. But money is merely a faith-based claim on the essentials necessary to support human life. And what is at the bottom of that pyramid of essentials, propping up everything that makes life worth living? Those humble little specks of germplasm, capable of bringing forth life from bare soil.

All of this helps explain why the battle for domination of the global seed trade has reached a fever pitch in recent years. The route to this battle was charted long ago, with the forming of ASTA and the subsequent dissolution of the USDA seed distribution program. Certainly, it was confirmed on June 16, 1980, with the landmark *Diamond v. Chakrabarty* ruling and, more quietly that same year, with the introduction of the Bayh-Dole Act. Over the 3 decades since then, the battle has only increased in pace and ferocity.

The next major skirmish was launched on June 7, 1995, when the US Patent and Trademark Office received a patent application from Monsanto (yep, them again) that began with a nearly indecipherable sentence: *"A method for making a genetically modified plant comprising regenerating a whole plant from a plant cell that has been transfected with DNA sequences comprising a first gene whose expression results in an altered plant phenotype linked to a transiently active promoter, the gene and promoter being separated by a blocking sequence flanked on either side by specific excision sequences, a second gene that encodes a recombinase specific for the specific excision sequences linked to a repressible promoter, and a third gene that encodes the repressor specific for the repressible promoter."*

In plain English, this was an application for a seed technology known officially as genetic use restriction technology (GURT) and unofficially as "suicide seed." When applied, GURT is the plant equivalent of neutering: The plant will grow, but it will never produce offspring. Its seeds will be sterile.

Why does this matter? Because suicide seed eliminates the ability of farmers to save their own seed from year to year. Indeed, it makes them utterly dependent on the seed manufacturer, year in, year out. Now, it's true that hybridized seed has led to effectively the same outcome, but there are two important points to consider: First, hybrid seed *can* be saved, even if the results are far from guaranteed. From a simple food security standpoint, it's enormously preferable to have something to plant, even if you're not exactly sure what the outcome will be. Second, not every farmer uses hybrid seed. In fact, the Canadian wheat industry relies on saved seed for an estimated 90 percent of its crop. Suicide seed would cost Canadian wheat farmers an extra $100 million annually. And consider the estimated 1.4 billion people globally who primarily rely on saved seed to provide their nourishment. These are mostly small-scale subsistence farmers in developing countries; they simply don't have the money to purchase seed every year. GURT would be nothing short of a death knell for them.

The global outcry over suicide seed technology was immediate and overwhelming, and in 1999, Monsanto made a public commitment not to implement GURT. But the statement concluded with a sentence that should send chills through anyone concerned about corporate control over our food: "Monsanto does not rule out the potential development and use of this technology in the future." In other words, Monsanto does not rule out the potential to assume absolute control over a large percentage of the global food supply.

Still, even as GURT remains tenuously under wraps, the consolidation continues unabated. On January 24, 2005, Monsanto parted with a cool $1.4 billion to buy Seminis, a company that controlled 40 percent of the US vegetable seed market and supplied the genetics for 55 percent of the lettuce, 75 percent of the tomatoes, and 85 percent of the peppers on supermarket shelves. In other words, if you had a salad during the first weeks of 2005 or at any point prior, you almost surely had a Seminis product on your plate. Now, of course, that same salad exists at the behest of Monsanto.

This is a lot of information about an industry you've likely never considered, and we haven't even talked about genetically modified organisms yet. GMOs are organisms (in our case, seeds) that have had their genetic material altered in a laboratory. In seeds, genetic modification is sort of like artificial hybridization; the technology is typically used to inscribe a particular variety with the ability to weather nutrient-deficient soil, or to survive increased density per acre, or to shrug off the effects of chemical pesticides and herbicides. This has been a particular boon to Monsanto, whose triple-stack corn—which combines Roundup Ready technology (in other words, it resists damage from Roundup herbicide, which, rather conveniently, is also a Monsanto product) with YieldGard Corn Borer and Yield-Gard Rootworm insect controls—leads the US corn market. Depending on the year, GMO seeds account for about 85 percent of all corn planted, 90 percent of all soybeans, and approximately 90 percent of all upland cotton.

Why is this a problem? Well, according to Monsanto, it's not: "There is no need for, or value in testing the safety of GM foods in humans. So long as the introduced protein is determined safe, food from GM crops determined to be substantially equivalent is not expected to pose any health risks," reads a portion of a statement on the company's Web site.

Not everyone is so sanguine concerning the safety of GM crops. A study published in a late-2009 edition of the *International Journal of Biological Sciences* showed a correlation between organ damage in rats (primarily to the kidney and liver, but also to the heart, adrenal glands, spleen, and hematopoietic stem cells that live in bone marrow) and Monsanto's genetically modified corn. Ironically, the data supporting these findings were drawn from a study sponsored by Monsanto in 2005. The study was kept confidential until Greenpeace obtained a court order for its publication and funded the first statistical analysis of the data.

Let us make a quick accounting of the issues relating to seed. First, for all practical matters, very few of us know anything about it. We don't know how to cultivate it or how to save it. (An increasing minority, at least, know how to plant it; in 2009, an estimated 43 million Americans kept a garden, up from 36 million the year before. A recession, it seems, provides ample incentive to get your hands dirty.) Perhaps even more problematic: Few of us have even considered that we *should* know anything about seed. It is the ultimate "unknown unknown," which is more than a little disconcerting, considering that it is a cornerstone of modern civilization.

Second, we are entirely dependent on a handful of profit-driven multinational corporations for the seed necessary to grow our nation's food. If you're even slightly suspicious, you might wonder if the lack of competition explains why the price of Monsanto seeds has been on a bit of a tear of late. In 2009, the company raised some corn seed prices by 25 percent; the projected increase in 2010 was a more reasonable 7 percent. In 2009, soy farmers fared even worse: Their seed prices rose by 28 percent. Still, they caught a break in '10, when prices were expected to jump by less than 6 percent. But even absent the issue of price controls, I think we should be asking ourselves a simple question: Is it really in our best interests to have a handful of corporations presiding over such a large and important component of our well-being?

Third, the largest of these companies holds a patent for a seed technology that would make it impossible for farmers to save its seed from year to year. To be sure, even without GURT, the horse has pretty much left the stable when it comes to seed saving. The commoditization of seed is all but complete, and our dependence on corporate seed is just that: a dependence. But the symbolism of seeds that grow into neutered plants is a stark reminder of how reliant we've become and how ruthless we've been in the pursuit of profits-by-agriculture. After all, it is the nature of plants to reproduce; depriving them of that ability by dint of genetic tinkering seems a cruel application of science. To anyone who believes in humanity's right to feed itself, the very fact that GURT exists and that the globe's largest seed producer "does not rule out the potential development and use of this technology in the future" should be worth a few restless nights. GURT effectively turns seed into a nonrenewable resource; it dismantles the final barrier between the corporation and the public's right to provide for itself.

Fourth, corn and soybeans grown from genetically modified seed (which account for 85 and 89 percent, respectively, of all corn and soybeans grown in the United States) have recently been shown to cause organ damage in rats. Now, I am not a rat; neither, presumably, are you. But rats are typically used in these types of experiments in large part because, as mammals, their reactions to a given study serve as a fairly strong indicator of how the human body would respond. (Yes, other mammals could serve, but rats have the poor fortune to be willing breeders, easy keepers, and have a maligned place in our culture.)

Fifth, the consolidation of our seed industry has resulted in "genetic erosion" in the germplasm (*germplasm* is the collection of genetic resources that make up an organism) that feeds the world. The Food and Agriculture Organization of the United Nations estimates that since 1900, approximately 75 percent of the genetic diversity of agricultural crops has been lost. From a purely economical view, the reasoning seems clear: As biotechnology continues its relentless march toward varieties that produce ever-greater yields, why maintain germplasm that can no longer compete? Simply to maintain diversity?

Well, yeah, that's actually a very good idea, as first illustrated over 150 years ago during the greatest crop failure the world has known to date: the Irish potato famine. Turns out the Irish potato farmers had unanimously relied on seed stock from potatoes that had originated in the Andes mountains of South America and, as such, had not developed resistance to a regional fungus that reduced yields by as much as 75 percent over many growing seasons. At the time, the Irish were entirely dependent on potatoes as a staple food; the blight caused the starvation of more than a million people. Closer to home, and a bit more recently, a case of southern corn leaf blight hit the Corn Belt of the United States in 1970, reducing yields by an average of 15 percent. Ninety percent of the corn hybrids available at the time were susceptible, as they shared the same plant cell cytoplasm.

Crop failures are a simple fact of agricultural life, even in an era of engineered germplasm. The summer of 2009 was a particularly bad one for tomatoes and potatoes in the Northeast, when a late blight caused by *Phytophthora infestans* (charming name, eh?) blew through the region. And I use the word "blew" literally: One of the dangers of these infections is that they can travel for miles on the wind, hopscotching from farm to farm, withering leaves and blackening fruits. Potato and tomato farmers through the region lost entire crops.

Now, the regional loss of a summer's worth of heirloom tomatoes does not a famine make. And it would be disingenuous to suggest that these growers could simply have planted another variety to escape the ravages of late blight. For starters, by the time the blight showed up, it was too late to sow another crop. And there's no telling if the second crop would have resisted the blight. But an underlying truth remains: In the face of crop disease, particularly the sort of multiyear afflictions that can lead to true and lasting hunger, genetic diversity is your ally.

Perhaps you can see why the whole subject was starting to bring me down a bit. Why, in only a few months' time, I'd gone from rarely (if ever) thinking about seed to wondering if perhaps we stand on the cusp of agricultural Armageddon, courtesy of our collective ignorance and shortsightedness in relinquishing all control of the germplasm that feeds us. It's as if we looked around for the very thing that is most crucial to keeping us alive, handed over the rights to its production and replication to a for-profit multinational corporation, and then spent billions of dollars each year buying it back from them. Actually, it's not "as if" we did these things, because we *did* do them. Which made me think two things: *What the hell were we thinking?* And, *I could really use some good news.*

So I went to Waterville, Maine. This was not as irrational a response as you might be thinking, which most likely is: *What the hell does Waterville, Maine, have to do with good seed news?* The answer to that question can be found by taking, as I did on an early March day in 2010, the first left past the Burger King on Waterville's main drag onto a short, dead-end street, where a gray colonial in the middle stages of terminal decline will quickly come into view. On the day of my visit, there was no lawn to speak of, and what with the fast-food joint almost next door, the rotting porch roof, and the vaguely abandoned look of the house, the place cast an aura of dilapidation bordering on despair. There was no sign on the door, but I was prepared for that, because CR Lawn, the founder and president of Fedco Seeds, had told me not to expect one. So I parked my Subaru, walked over a patch of cracked pavement, and gingerly stepped across the porch.

Unless you're an avid gardener, I'd be surprised if you've heard of Fedco Seeds. It's a modestly sized company (about $3.6 million annually) and it caters to a particular niche of diverse, small-scale vegetable growers, primarily those producing for their own home or for a local market. Of the crops growing in our one-quarter acre of gardens on our small farm in Vermont, about half origi-nated at Fedco; the other half comes from High Mowing Organic Seeds, which is an even smaller company than Fedco and one that specializes in organic, GMO-free seed. Conveniently enough, High Mowing is situated only a few miles down the road from our Vermont home, close enough that we typically pick up our annual order at the company's warehouse.

The seed business is built on niches, and while companies like Monsanto, Syngenta, and DuPont own the industrial niche, which in turn owns the overwhelming majority of the food produced in this country, the other end of the spectrum— that catering to home gardeners and small-scale vegetable farmers—is populated by small businesses like High Mowing and Fedco, each seeking their own slice of the pie. In the case of High Mowing, it's the slice that is unwaveringly committed to organic agriculture, to the point where even their seeds must be produced according to the standards that define organic. At Fedco, organic seed accounts for a significant portion of sales (38 percent, to be exact), but the overriding vibe exuded by the company's funky black-and-white catalogs and annual letter from CR Lawn is of a broader antiestablishment nature.

I found Lawn in his office, which was—how to say it?—very much not fully clean. It contained, in no particular order, a can of 3-in-One oil, a mostly eaten bowl of popcorn drowning in nutritional yeast, an empty bottle of Twisted Tea, and a roll of toilet paper. Clearly, CR's office is a place of many and varied pursuits, some of which I didn't care to know more about. The drop ceiling above Lawn's desk boasted a large water stain and a darker, substantive growth that bore a striking resemblance to mold. There were numerous metal filing cabinets that looked as if they were waiting for the 1950s to call and demand their immediate return. A bumper sticker pinned to the wall read: "Oh well, I wasn't using my civil liberties anyway."

CR Lawn is 64. He sported a wispy gray beard, narrow-rimmed eyeglasses, and less than a full complement of teeth. On the day I visited, he was wearing a purple sweatshirt and a pair of sweatpants; neither appeared to have seen the inside of a washing machine in quite some time. Tufts of his beard stuck straight out from the sides of his face, partially obscuring his ears. I was reminded, vaguely, of Gandalf, the wizard from Tolkien's *Lord of the Rings* trilogy.

CR's given name is Paul, but it's been decades since anyone close to him has used it. The moniker was bestowed in high school, when he ran for president of the student government

under the slogan "The grass grows greener on Paul's lawn." In
the circuitous logic of teenagers, CR came to stand for crabgrass:
Crab Grass Lawn. "My best filter for telephone solicitors is if
they use my given name," CR told me. He was standing by his
desk, rocking back and forth softly, shifting his weight from one
foot to the other and back again. I thought maybe there was
something in my manner or questioning that was making him
nervous, and I asked if this were so. "I might rock a little when
we're talking," he told me. "But it doesn't really mean anything."

After a brief tour of the offices (a half-dozen or so people
work in the Waterville office; the bulk of Fedco's employees
spend their working hours at the company's warehouse facility
in nearby Clinton), CR and I prepared to walk a few blocks into
downtown Waterville to a coffee shop he frequents. It was early
March, and CR slipped two more soiled sweatshirts over his
head to gird him against the chill. The second was hooded; one
drawstring hung almost to his waist; the other didn't even clear
the bottom of his beard. I suppose CR could have made a con-
scious effort to appear more disheveled, but I'm not certain he
would have succeeded.

Waterville, Maine, is a faded industrial town of about 16,000,
situated about 45 minutes from the state's rocky central coast
and about 90 minutes north of Portland. It is perched at the
junction of the Kennebec and Sebasticook Rivers, once major
trading routes for the Native American and early European set-
tler populations. Its location helped establish the municipality
as a strong industrial base in the early 1900s, but like so many
American cities built on manufacturing, Waterville has not
fared particularly well. Over the past few decades, its mills and

factories have closed one by one, bowing to foreign competition and a populace seduced by the bargain-basement price tags attached to the goods produced in far-off countries. In 2008, the town's median household income was $34,000, compared to the statewide average of $46,000. At 9:00 on the morning I arrived, only two storefronts along Waterville's short downtown business district appeared to be open: a coffeehouse and a pawnshop. And there were a lot more people in the pawnshop. "Waterville's on its way back," CR told me, as we strolled toward his favorite coffeehouse. From what I'd observed, this seemed an overly optimistic view of things.

At the café, after procuring coffee and bagels, CR and I sat and he recounted his upbringing on a 25-acre farm in Cornwall, Vermont, a small town near the shores of Lake Champlain. His parents, Irwin and Rose, had purchased the farm in 1940; they were living on Long Island at the time, but ripe with the expectation that the second act of the Great Depression was imminent. As such, they spent much of their free time in Vermont, doing all they could to prepare the farm for the self-sufficiency they believed would be necessitated by a protracted period of economic malaise. "My mother was a communist and my father was a fellow traveler," CR explained. "They believed the commie analysis that the only way out of the Great Depression was World War II." He was rocking slightly in his chair; little crumbs of bagel and dots of cream cheese swung on his beard.

From Vermont, the family moved to upstate New York, where Irwin had received another teaching job and CR grew into a young man, eventually attending Oberlin, a small liberal arts college in Oberlin, Ohio. "I learned more outside the classroom at

Oberlin than in," he told me. "I went in conservative and came out leftie. Of course, the Vietnam War had something to do with that."

CR continued his education at Yale, in pursuit of a law degree and the political future that might go with it. "At that point, I wanted to go into politics." His expression turned incredulous at his own naïveté. "A more unsuitable person for politics I don't think you could ever find." Still, owing largely to the persistent pleading of Irwin and Rose, CR did earn a Yale law degree in 1971. "It has come in useful at Fedco," he noted. It sounded almost like a confession.

Following graduation, CR spent a winter in Eldora, Colorado, holing up at 8,700 feet in a cabin and "trying to figure out what to do with the rest of my life." It took him 9 months to burn through his $300 savings, by which point he'd plotted his future: He'd return to New England and establish a homestead. To hell with politics.

In Canaan, Maine, CR bought 60 acres for $4,000 and quickly joined with a small group of friends to form a commune of sorts. He built two cabins, a process he deems "the hardest thing I've ever done in my life. I didn't even know how to hammer an 8-penny nail." The cabins are still standing, although at the time of my visit, CR was in the final stages of selling his share in the property to the remaining community members. Like most 1970s-era back-to-the-landers, CR became involved with the local food cooperative. Unlike most '70s-era back-to-the-landers, CR actually found himself living in a food cooperative warehouse. "My cabin didn't have insulation, and I only had a cookstove for heat. All I was doing was struggling to stay warm." CR approached the Maine Federation of Co-ops and made them a generous, if desperate, offer: If they'd let him stay in the heated warehouse, he'd work for $75 per month. A deal was struck, and CR bedded down among bags of wheat berries and tubs of organic peanut butter.

During this period, CR learned something extremely interesting about seed: It can be purchased cheaply in bulk quantities. "I learned that I could buy a pound of beet seed for about $5." Remember, a packet of seed weighs only a fraction of an ounce (in the case of beet seed, it's typically 1/16 ounce), and in today's dollars, costs between two and three bucks. Even accounting for inflation, the markup is obvious and drastic. And, it should be noted, not unfair: It requires a good bit of work to divide a pound of seed into 250 or so packets.

Still, CR saw an opportunity to significantly reduce the cost of seed for co-op members, and he began purchasing seed in bulk to divvy up into smaller, home-gardener-size packets. It was all very informal at first, but it didn't take long for CR to view this arrangement as a business prospect, and in 1979, Fedco Seeds was launched. "I projected 100 orders for a total of $10,000," CR told me. "We had 98 orders for a total of $10,000." CR has always had a way with numbers, either predicting them or visualizing them or simply working with them. "I can beat a calculator," he told me, so of course I challenged him to a calculator race: "What's 363 times 278?" I asked, keying in the numbers. CR focused his gaze on the ceiling: "100,914." He said it calmly and confidently, as if there could be no doubt as to his accuracy. Indeed, he was correct and only about a single second slower than the calculator. "I'm almost an idiot savant," he said, looking proud as can be. For the first time, I noticed that one of the nose pads on his eyeglasses was bent and, rather than lying along the length of his nose as it was designed to do, stuck straight out, like an accusatory finger. How it wasn't driving him mad was beyond me.

In 3 years, Fedco's sales grew by a factor of five. Suddenly, CR had a career. Things leveled off during the early-80s recession. Then the business began to grow again, by a handful of percentage points each year. In 1998, Fedco finally began accepting credit card payments, just in time to manage the 30 percent annual growth that prefaced Y2K. (CR still does not carry a credit card. No cell phone, either.)

To CR, the influx of seed orders in 1999 was a lesson in how his company's sales could serve to gauge the broader social mood and even predict economic contractions. When times are bad, or when people believe times are about to turn bad, they do just what CR's parents had done: try to secure the means by which to feed their family. And a big part of that is seed.

So when Fedco's sales began to explode in 2007, eventually increasing by 50 percent over 2 years, CR took note. "It was the first thing that clued me in that something serious was happening. I was sitting in this very café, thinking about the fact that seed orders were coming in like I'd never seen before, and it just seemed like things were really weird." So weird that CR was compelled to sell the stock he'd inherited from his father. "I sold almost at the peak." "All of it?" I asked. "All of it." He looked nearly as pleased as when he'd raced the calculator.

These days, Fedco is a $3.6 million enterprise, 60 percent of which is owned by its customers; 40 percent is owned by employees. Eighty percent of profits is funneled back into the company; the other 20 percent is redistributed to customers based on their purchase history. (Every year, my family receives a check from Fedco as part of our "ownership" dividend. It typically amounts to five or six bucks.) "To me, a co-op is sort of a halfway house for recovering socialists and capitalists," says CR. "The thing I love about co-ops is that there's no owner or profiteering. The thing I don't love is if they insist on consensus. I think you have to have managers and power relationships, even though I couldn't draw you a diagram of what Fedco's power relationship looks like."

Not surprisingly, CR has strong opinions regarding the broader seed industry, which he views as dangerously consolidated and centralized. And which, by virtue of its need to purchase seed in large quantities, Fedco is largely dependent on. In a sense, small seed companies like Fedco are really in the business of repackaging: They purchase lots of seed from independent contractors and larger enterprises, which they then break down into smaller packets and sell to growers. Their ability to thrive is based on how they define their niche and how successfully they market to it rather than their skill at producing seed.

This arrangement presented a challenge in 2005, when Monsanto purchased Seminis, which at the time was Fedco's largest single supplier, providing 70 of 900 varietals. CR immediately penned a letter to Fedco customers, asking whether or not the company should continue distributing Seminis seed. The response was a resounding "no," and Fedco unceremoniously dumped the Seminis varieties, some of which have still not been replaced. "Seminis was a great company, and it was very hard to let go of them. But ethically it was the right thing to do, and it ended up being a brilliant marketing move, because it really identified who we are and what we stand for." Still, it was a bittersweet moment in Fedco history. "Seminis had the best tomato genetics. There's almost no place to go for decent tomato genetics anymore." An almost wistful look fell across his face. Of course, there *is* a place to go for decent tomato genetics; it just happens to be Monsanto.

CR doesn't have a problem with Monsanto per se. And Fedco still purchases bulk seed from Syngenta, the world's third-largest purveyor of seed and one that holds licensing agreements with Monsanto. In total, Fedco buys seed from upwards of 50 growers, ranging from Syngenta, with its $11 billion annual revenue, to a Maine woman who grows melon seed in her backyard. Because many of its customers care deeply about where their seed comes from, Fedco codes each of the varieties it offers by supplier, ranging from regional seed farmers to multinationals engaged in genetic engineering. "I think there's room for everybody. Monsanto could stay around for all I care; the reason we boycotted them is because they're too dominant. They want to control the world!" A fleck of cream cheese popped out of his mouth and landed in his beard. He dropped his voice a decibel or two and leaned forward. "I'm getting to the point where I think the major enemy is centralization. I want decentralization, I want heirloom varieties, I want hybrids. I want the whole gamut."

This all sounded well and good to me, but it doesn't exactly add up to an overthrow of a globalized, hyperconsolidated seed industry. It doesn't turn back the clock on the for-profit privatization of germplasm—the very foundation of our food supply—that now holds us captive. Even, to a certain extent,

CR Lawn and his little antiestablishment seed company. It doesn't restore the thousands of plant varieties that have been allowed to lapse into extinction. It doesn't make Monsanto's terminator seed patent null and void.

CR Lawn knows all this. He knows that Fedco isn't so much a solution as a bandage. But he's not afraid to imagine the ways in which that bandage could be replicated to create a seed industry built from hundreds of small-scale, regionalized producers that specialize in broadly different varieties evolved to a time and place. "Plants and seeds are alive. They're constantly changing. The Kentucky pole beans we're selling now are not the same as they were 100 years ago, and in 100 years, they won't be the same as they are now. If you took the same variety and grew it in different ecosystems for 20 years, they're going to be very different plants."

He's not afraid to use his company as a pulpit from which to shine some light into the dark and dirty recesses of the seed industry. "There's a tradition in the industry that you don't talk negatively about the industry or your products. Frankly, I don't go along with that." He leaned forward another inch or two, and dropped his voice to a whisper. "I think it's time to stop being so nice."

A few days after my visit with CR Lawn, I stood in the front yard of our northern Vermont home. It was mid-March; the ground was frozen and dormant under a thick blanket of snow, but the air carried a welcome breath of spring. The sun shone brightly, and the temperature had risen above freezing for the first time in many days. I wore only a T-shirt and jeans, which was ridiculous—goose bumps abounded—but when you're emerging from 3 months of hard, sunless weather and nature throws you a bone. . . . Well, that's just what you do.

I may have been bare armed, but I was not empty handed. A minute or two earlier, standing over my kitchen sink, I'd poured an entire packet of seed into my left hand. Specifically, it was carrot seed; more specifically still, it was of a variety known as Scarlet Nantes or, more formally, *Daucus carota* subsp. *sativus*. My wife had purchased the seed from High Mowing Organic Seeds, which, as I've mentioned, is headquartered only a handful of miles to the west of our home. The fact that I live within a 15-minute drive of a seed company puts me in very rare company: It's difficult to get an accurate count of all the cottage industry seed suppliers in the United States, but it's safe to say the number is best measured in dozens rather than in hundreds.

The seeds in my hand weighed so little—$\frac{1}{32}$ ounce, to be exact, or a bit less than 1 gram—that I might easily have forgotten they were there. They were tiny, small enough that it was difficult to pick up a single seed. They looked like inconsequential flecks of something you'd brush off your shirt; the remnants of a poppy seed bagel eaten in haste, perhaps. I stood there for a bit, waiting. My family was gone, and our home is far back from the road; there was no one in sight, and I did not feel self-conscious standing in the snow in a T-shirt with a handful of carrot seeds. I was cold, sure, but I could wait.

I heard it and saw it before I felt it: a gust of wind. The treetops along the northern fringe of our land began to sway. I counted a few beats, until I could feel the push of air against my skin. Then, with as much vigor as I could muster, I hurled my handful of seeds into the air.

Oh, how I yearn to recount the glorious manner in which my seeds took flight on the late-winter wind. I long to tell you how they caught a current and rode it for miles before landing inconspicuously in the snow, where they would wait patiently for spring with the rest of us. And I wish I could say that months later, when carrot tops began to emerge from the ground all over my little town, and my neighbors were puzzling over whom to thank for this unexpected bounty, I humbly came forth to accept their gratitude.

That is not exactly what happened. The truth is, the seeds didn't go far. In fact, most of them blew back into my face and hair, where they became hopelessly ensnared. And now I *did* feel self-conscious. For a few minutes, I'd fancied myself a sort of 21st-century Johnny Appleseed, setting my gift of carrot seed adrift on the wind. I liked this image of myself; it made me feel both benevolent and resourceful. Take it from me: Shaking seeds out of your hair is a good way to lower the curtain on visions of self-grandeur.

Still, I knew enough about seed to recognize that the diminutive nature of the *Daucus carota* subsp. *sativus* I'd ineffectually scattered about our yard belies its innate toughness. Somewhere, somehow, I was certain that at least a few of those seeds would eventually find favorable conditions. Bare soil. Sunlight. Enough but not too much rain. Slowly, the embryo inside the seedpods would swell with water, and a tiny filament of root would emerge, anchoring the fledgling plant. Soon, a fragile sprout would surface, reaching for the light.

I turned and walked back toward the house. By now, I was really quite cold.

10

The surveillance camera hanging from the ceiling of the Raw-some Foods warehouse in Venice, California, is pretty much the same as surveillance cameras hanging from the ceilings of businesses across North America. It is small and black and does what a surveillance camera is supposed to do: silently record the comings and goings of anyone who passes through the warehouse doorway.

But unlike so many surveillance cameras, which are intended to protect a business from thievery or other malicious acts perpetrated by members of the general public, the camera at Raw-some is there for an entirely different purpose: to document a potential raid by state or federal authorities.

Indeed, that is exactly what happened on June 30, 2010, at almost exactly 8:00 a.m., when the door to the warehouse swung open to admit four officers sent by the Los Angeles County District Attorney's office. The officers entered slowly and fanned out across the room. Their guns were drawn, and their heads were bent and tilted to afford a better view down

the short barrels of their pistols. To my admittedly inexperi-
enced eye, informed by drug bust and bank robber gang appre-
hension scenes in movie and television, it seemed like classic
police invasion technique. Hell, if I'd been busting down that
door with gun in hand, it's exactly what I would have done, figuring that at any moment, some ne'er-do-well might pop out of
a closet, finger on the trigger of his black market AK-47. *Kill or
be killed. Go ahead, punk: Make my day.*

Except that, well, Rawsome's not really that sort of place.
Actually, it's not even close to being that sort of place. Because
Rawsome is . . . you might want to sit down for this . . . a grocery store. As the officers moved through the warehouse, guns
and eyes scanning every nook and cranny for the criminal element, they were forced to navigate around bins of what appear
to be mixed vegetables. The video is a little grainy, so it's a bit
hard to make out exactly what kinds of vegetables, but I'm
pretty sure I saw some broccoli. Or maybe it was cabbage. It
was something green, anyway, piled in one of those waxed
cardboard boxes vegetables are often shipped in.

I know what you're thinking: Rawsome must have been a
front, the legal entity for some sort of money-laundering
scheme, or simply a distraction from the gambling, moon-
shine, drugs, and prostitution that unfolded in a windowless
room beyond the boxes of cabbage or broccoli or whatever the
hell it was. Except that wasn't the case either. No, the reason
the LA County district attorney's office had such a keen, gun-
wielding interest in Rawsome wasn't because of activities
being carried out under the cover of food: It was because of the
food itself.

Which makes this an appropriate place to explain that although Rawsome is merely a grocery store, it probably isn't like any grocery story you've ever shopped in. Rawsome exists to provide its customers with foods that are raw. (You might have figured that out by now; the name *is* a bit of a giveaway.) And those foods are, in many cases, illegal. Raw milk. Raw cheese, aged for fewer than the 60 days required by the FDA. Almonds that have not been pasteurized, as has been the US law since 2007. You know, that sort of stuff.

To understand why such an establishment exists, we need to back up to Chapter 6, where we learned that a diverse population of gut microbes might well be key to vibrant health and perhaps even imbue us with a degree of protection from bacteria that would otherwise do us harm. What's more, we need to understand that raw milk consumers do not have an exclusive on the claim to microbial and enzymatic diversity in their favorite food. Indeed, one of the fastest-growing food movements in the United States is defined by a contingent of people whose desire to eat raw food goes far beyond their milk to the fruit, vegetables, nuts, dairy, and in some cases even the meat they consume.

Now, diet extremism is nothing new to modern American culture. As Michael Pollan has correctly pointed out, we live in an era of almost paralyzing confusion regarding how and what we should feed ourselves. Anyone old enough to be reading this book has lived at least some of his or her life in the era of nutritive turmoil; that many of us don't even recognize this turmoil is indicative of how pervasive it has become. We don't think of it as turmoil; we think of it as *normal*. It is almost impossible to imagine that not so long ago, Americans weren't obsessed with diet. The turning point isn't hard to identify: It was the early 1960s, when cholesterol began taking the rap for heart disease. It didn't hurt that the obesity rate was barely a third of what it is now; we had not yet become a society diseased by excess body weight. And so people ate what they liked, and what they liked was usually a reflection of how they'd been fed as children. In other words, there was still a degree of "food ancestry" in our culture.

The age of nutrition pretty much did away with all that, as we learned that saturated fats are killing us (or are they?), that high levels of cholesterol in our blood put us at extreme risk for heart disease (or do they?), that eating a low-fat, high-carb diet is the best way to maintain a healthy weight (or is it?), and that margarine and other engineered foodlike substances are the cornerstone of a well-balanced diet. In recent years, studies have begun to refute these findings, leaving us more uncertain than ever about what to eat. It's enough to make a fellow want to do something crazy, like fill his freezer with a road-killed deer and a couple dozen pounds of dumpstered cheese.

Or, perhaps, shop at Rawsome. Now, in the interest of fairness in the context of my previous commentary on dietary fads, I feel compelled to point out that eating raw foods isn't exactly the new, new thing. After all, there once was life without fire. In other words, eating raw foods—yes, including meat—wasn't always considered dangerous. It wasn't illegal to produce or distribute raw foods, and gnawing on an uncooked haunch of animal flesh wasn't merely a stupid party trick. Because it was the norm.

The revival of the raw foods diet in the modern era owes much to a fellow named Aris LaTham. LaTham is a tall, slender African American in his sixties; he was born in Panama but immigrated to the United States, where, in 1979, he launched Sunfired Foods, a raw food business based in Harlem. He wears his hair in long, thin dreadlocks, maintains a fluffy white beard, and, if the photos on the Sunfired Web site are any indication, owns at least one purple sports jacket that he likes to wear buttoned low, his gleaming chest on proud display. It very much looks as if it might be waxed (his chest, not the jacket).

Like most raw foodists, LaTham believes that the enzymes in uncooked foods aid digestion and that these foods are teeming with beneficial microbes. And, contend LaTham and the growing legion of raw foodists, it's not merely that raw foods are healthful, it's that cooked foods are downright dangerous. This runs counter to pretty much every piece of advice from every food regulatory body that exists or has ever existed, but there is some science behind these claims. Ironically, this is particularly true in relation to the cooking of meat, which has been shown to release carcinogenic compounds during heating, especially at high temperatures. One study conducted by researchers at the National Cancer Institute found that people who ate beef rare or medium-rare had less than one-third the risk of stomach cancer than those who ate beef medium-well or well-done.

But it's not merely meat, or heat, that draws the ire of raw foodists. They contend that food additives such as preservatives, flavor enhancers, colorings, and other laboratory-concocted ingredients are not part of a healthy diet. Ditto stimulants and depressants, such as alcohol, tobacco, or black tea. Coffee?

Forget about it. And raw foodists tend to avoid, like the plague (or crispy bacon), added sugars. Most raw foodists are strict vegetarians, and many of those are vegans, consuming no animal products at all.

Frankly, I have a hard time getting too worked up about such a diet, but maybe that's because I haven't tried it and experienced the amazing, nearly boundless energy and sense of well-being it supposedly confers. I say "supposedly" because, like I said, I haven't tried eating this way, and there's scant research on the subject. So, like you, I really only have the testimony of LaTham and the burgeoning population of raw food devotees.

In any event, other than being one of the modern raw foods movement's forefathers, LaTham has nothing to do with Rawsome, which was founded by a 63-year-old raw food devotee named James Stewart. Stewart is one of the protagonists of Los Angeles County's raw foods movement; back in the '90s, before it was legal to distribute unpasteurized milk in LA County, Stewart was bringing it into the city in the trunk of his old Mazda. He'd make the 5-hour drive north to what was then the state's only raw milk dairy and return with a car full of milky contraband, which he distributed among his friends and the handful of health food stores willing to break the law.

Stewart's affinity for raw foods is the result of his introduction in 1997 to the dietary beliefs of a man called Aajonus Vonderplanitz, which is the sort of name that makes me wish my parents had spent a bit more time considering all their options. As you might expect of someone with such a moniker, he lives in Malibu, California, where he is probably the 38th Aajonus Vonderplanitz in the phone book.

I'm going to sidetrack a little here, because the story of Aajonus Vonderplanitz is simply too good to ignore. This is in part because, unlike the majority of raw foodists, Vonderplanitz is a profligate consumer of raw meat, including fish, beef, chicken, and pork.

Wait a moment: *chicken and pork?* I was raised to believe, fervently, in the restorative powers of a rare hamburger or steak, and being a worldly fellow, 1 have dined at restaurants where uncooked fish was served. But I'd been taught—as surely you must have been—that chicken and pork should always be cooked to the utmost doneness. To ignore this mandate was to risk a slow, agonizing death by . . . well, actually, I never did figure out why these particular species were so dangerous. But the implied threat was enough, and despite my fondness for bloody beef, I have always cooked chicken and pork to at least 160°F, and usually a good bit more.

Back to Aajonus and his unusual story. As a boy, Aajonus suffered from numerous conditions, including dyslexia and autism; these afflictions were exacerbated by an older brother who tortured him almost daily. His father was a strict disciplinarian and put Aajonus in the hospital on numerous occasions. Around his 10th birthday, Aajonus developed peritonitis, an inflammation of the tissue that lines the wall of the abdomen and covers the abdominal organs. His doctor misdiagnosed his stomach pains as appendicitis before discovering that his appendix was just fine. It was removed anyway.

During this period, Aajonus's bones were brittle, and he broke numerous appendages. He was diagnosed as borderline diabetic at 13; at 15, he was diagnosed with juvenile diabetes. His 15th year was a bad one indeed, because he also developed angina pectoris muscle spasms in and around the heart.

Things quieted down for a few years (one can only imagine his doctor's relief), but the respite was short lived, because at 19, Aajonus developed an ulcer that turned tumorous after surgery. It was irradiated, but the treatment caused him to develop multiple myeloma, a cancer of the white blood cells that is generally considered incurable. Chemo was prescribed, and after 3 months of treatment, Aajonus refused to continue. He prepared himself for death.

Fortunately for Aajonus, his luck was about to take a turn for the better: As he lay about the house, waiting for the reaper to come calling, a hospice volunteer slipped him a book written by a woman who'd cured herself of cancer by drinking raw carrot juice. Aajonus considered his options and decided that carrot juice wasn't so bad. So he started drinking raw carrot juice, and within 10 days, his dyslexia had gone away. For his entire life, dyslexia had kept him from reading; now he began to devour books, mostly about diets and nutrition. Equally noteworthy was the fact that for the time being, at least, he didn't die.

Aajonus noticed that if he skipped a few days of carrot juice, his dyslexia returned. So he stopped skipping days and began experimenting with other radical diet-related treatments. The macrobiotic diet seemed to put the kibosh on his cancer but inflamed his diabetes and psoriasis. (I don't think I mentioned the psoriasis before; he had that, too.)

He kept tweaking his diet, convinced that if he got it right, he could reverse the conditions that had plagued him for the entirety of his young life. By the time he was 25, he was eating an entirely vegan raw foods diet. He felt better than he ever had, but he was often extremely hungry and would compensate for this by overeating until he vomited. Still, he had enough energy to climb on his bicycle and traverse North America, pedaling from coast to coast and from Alaska to Central America. He traveled light, sleeping on the ground or, when it rained, in trees (*in trees?*). He took much of his nourishment from the wild, foraging for berries and other edible plants. He was often in a state of euphoria, which he now attributes to mania caused by excessive consumption of fruit and its associated fructose.

Then his cancer returned. Again, Aajonus prepared to die; he simply didn't have any fight left in him. So he located a Native American burial ground, established a camp, and began to fast, expecting to starve himself to death. After a few weeks, he was scrawny but still alive and growing impatient with the whole process; at this rate, he'd be alive for another month. So when a coyote came into his camp with a dead rabbit and dropped it on his feet, Aajonus ate it. Not because he wanted food, but because he believed that wild rabbits harbor bacteria and viruses that would finally put an end to it all (he was probably thinking of the bacterium *Francisella tularensis*, which can indeed transmit from rabbits to humans but is not typically fatal). Aajonus settled in, secure in the knowledge that soon he would succumb to the effects of eating this raw, wild rodent. He closed his eyes and drifted into what he believed would be his final, forever sleep.

Imagine his surprise when he awoke the next morning feeling more refreshed than he had in years. He felt so good, in fact, that he no longer expected or even wanted to die. And damned if he wasn't pretty freakin' hungry. So he began hunting, eating whatever he could catch (rattlesnakes and songbirds featured prominently on his menu). Aajonus began roaming again, working on farms for foods like milk, cream, eggs, and meat. He still wasn't eating everything raw, but it was enough that soon he felt stronger than ever.

Aajonus returned to Los Angeles to spread the word about the dual miracle of raw foods and his improbable recovery. For the most part, people thought he was crazy (remember, we're talking about LA, so that's really saying something), but he pressed on and began experimenting with adding more raw meat to his diet. Still, he had lingering fears over foodborne illness and parasites, and so he limited his intake to just a couple servings of fish or chicken each week. Each time he ate raw meat, he felt as if he were rolling the dice and that, eventually, he'd be stricken.

It didn't happen. Instead, he felt stronger and stronger. He began running and doing pushups. He got a job working as the nutritionist at a health food store. People began commenting on his radiant appearance, and Aajonus excitedly explained that if only they would eat raw meat, too, they could look as good as he did. Most folks just nodded, but a few gave it a shot. Those who stuck with it told Aajonus stories of vastly improved health.

Yet Aajonus still couldn't shake the fear that raw meat would eventually make him sick. Much of his nervousness was due to the fact that during one of his surgeries, his vagus nerve had been severed; one of the functions of the vagus nerve is to regulate the stomach acid that kills potentially dangerous bacteria and parasites. The loss of his vagus also meant the loss of the acid, which put Aajonus in a particularly dangerous place in relation to foodborne illness. He continued eating meat anyway.

Then, when he was 35, Aajonus misidentified a wild mushroom and ended up ingesting an *Amanita phalloides*, aka "death cap." No one in written history had eaten even $\frac{1}{15}$ the amount he had and lived. Aajonus survived his little fungal snack, but not without some ramifications. His cancer returned with a vengeance, and his liver was nearly wiped out. His diabetes came back. He lost weight and suffered whole-body cramps. But he continued eating raw foods (although not mushrooms, presumably) and began to recover.

After 18 months of slow, incremental improvements in his health, Aajonus became frustrated, and eventually his frustration began to outweigh his fear of getting sick from eating raw meat. By this time, the guy was supposed to have died at least a half-dozen times, so perhaps it's no wonder he threw caution to the wind and began consuming raw animal flesh daily. Immediately, his diabetes vanished and his healing accelerated.

Over the years, Aajonus's nutritional counseling practice has grown, as has his success rate in healing his clients of chronic and often deadly disease. Through diet alone, Aajonus claims to have helped 232 out of 242 people put their cancers into remission; he claims this achievement was confirmed by a neuroscientist named Elnora Van Winkle. I did attempt to validate this claim, and while it is certainly true there was once a neuroscientist named Elnora Van Winkle, she died in 2001, making it difficult to reach her. Aajonus also credits his diet with turning him into something of a sexual master, able to enjoy as much as 6 hours of sex daily, with multiple orgasms. I absolutely did *not* attempt to validate this claim.

The story of how Aajonus Vonderplanitz came to be our nation's foremost proponent of eating raw meat is . . . how to put this . . . well, the word *incredulous* comes to mind. This is not to say it is untrue, only that if true, it represents perhaps the most unusual human health history I've ever encountered. Frankly, I did not expend much effort trying to verify or disprove Aajonus's story; my interest in him has more to do with the issue of food rights than his personal story. But at some point, I realized that, equally, I didn't *want* it to be untrue. It's such an outlandish story, so full of bad luck and bizarre medical redemption, that I wanted to believe in it, much in the same way I once wanted to believe in Santa Claus (you can imagine my dismay when, on my 30th birthday, my wife finally revealed that ole Saint Nick wasn't real). To fear the same fate for Aajonus's story reveals a fatal bias in my reporting, which I am attempting to mitigate somewhat by acknowledging it.

So, barring evidence to the contrary, I have chosen to take Aajonus at his word and have presented his story as if it were the gospel truth. Admittedly, his medical history and his path to raw foods have no bearing on the issue of food rights. And admittedly, his story is so outlandish that repeating it here might only discredit me and thus cast a pall over the rest of this book. I hope that is not the case, and that is why I present it in the spirit of entertainment only. If it's true . . . well, all I can say is Wow. Just *Wow*.

Which might explain why Aajonus has such a following and why he has attracted enough attention to gain a place on national network television espousing the benefits of raw meat. He appeared on *Ripley's Believe It or Not!* in 2002 (the episode was charmingly called "Rotten Meat Eater"); more recently, in a segment from the CBS show *The Doctors*, Aajonus can be seen eating raw chicken off the bone and noshing on uncooked hamburger. On the show, he also claims to have suffered 300 heart attacks by the age of 22, an assertion I had not previously turned up. He is short, but at 63 appears well built and exceptionally healthy. The best moment in the show is when Aajonus interrupts the doctor interviewing him to say, "I'm getting hungry," and then he proceeds to crack a raw egg against his teeth (nice touch, that one) before sucking it out of the shell. As the host delivers a "don't try this at home"-style disclaimer, the sounds of Aajonus's slurping can be heard in the background as he extracts the slimy remnants. Frankly, I can think of better ways to get people interested in eating raw eggs, but as a piece of theater, it works pretty darn well.

Back to James Stewart. By 2000, Stewart was illegally distributing raw milk to about 30 stores in LA County. That's an awful lot of raw milk to escape the attention of the county's health department. Indeed, by late in the year, the department's attention had been captured, and they pulled the milk from most of Stewart's outlets. So Stewart did the natural thing (well, "natural" if you're the sort of fellow willing to break the law in order to distribute raw milk): He began selling it out of a leased garage. "All of sudden, I had 20 or 30 people lining up every Wednesday and Saturday [he was open only on Wednesday and Saturday afternoons] waiting for the garage doors to open." Stewart called his business the *Raw Garage* and, for a period of about a year, operated without interference from the authorities.

In the meantime, Stewart, along with Vonderplanitz, with whom he'd become friends, successfully petitioned the county to change the laws pertaining to raw milk. With the product now fully legal to sell at the retail level, Stewart began importing milk from Mark McAfee's Organic Pastures dairy (he claims to have been the one who convinced McAfee to shift from selling organic milk intended for pasteurization to being a completely raw dairy) and distributing it to 89 stores in the county.

The Raw Garage was eventually shuttered by the authorities for lack of permits and other workspace violations. For a time, Stewart became a mobile raw milk crusader, selling out of a pair of refrigerated trucks in and around Venice. "I was the person who created the raw milk revolution in California," he told me. "Literally like a phoenix rising from the ashes." If there's anything I've learned about raw foodists, it's that they're fond of grandiose analogies. Stewart is no exception.

In 2005, Stewart and Vonderplanitz created an entity called Rawsome Foods, which would operate under the umbrella of Aajonus's organization, Right to Choose Healthy Food, founded in 1998. According to Stewart and Vonderplanitz, the structure of the organization allows it to operate without compliance with the plethora of licensing and labeling laws that normally preclude the sale and distribution of many raw food products. What RCHF does is craft lease agreements between its members and farmers, providing the former with the rights to the land and products of about 40 small farms across the United States. Basically, RCHF sidesteps the mandates attached to the act of selling food to the general citizenry by creating the legal framework whereby the consumers are no longer members of an unwitting public but instead act as owners of the products the farms produce. Therefore, claim Stewart and Vonderplanitz, as a members-only buying outlet, Rawsome does not fall under the purview of the FDA, the USDA, or anyone else who'd prefer it didn't exist. Instead, it is merely part of the lease agreement between members and farmers and is protected by over 80 years of precedent that equates leasing to ownership.

When Rawsome was founded, Stewart and Vonderplanitz crafted a letter outlining their intentions and beliefs and sent it to the LA County health department. "We were shocked that we didn't get a response," Stewart told me. "At least, we didn't until June 30, 2010." That's when agents from the FDA and FBI raided the building with guns drawn and, according to Stewart, hauled away thousands of dollars' worth of food, which was never returned.

There has been no mention of any illness related to Rawsome's products. Club members are required to sign a waiver acknowledging, in part, that 1) the food available there is not subjected to artificial temperatures above 99°F, dairy not below

42°F, and meats not below 38°F; 2) the food may contain microbes, including but not limited to salmonella, *E. coli*, campylobacter, listeria, gangrene, and parasites; 3) the eggs are unwashed and may have bacteria and poultry feces on them. There is also a paragraph in the waiver that reads: *"I fully understand that these features represent a different paradigm for food preparation, storage, and safety than those that are currently enforced by all local, state, and federal government agencies. As a member of this Club, I fully trust its administrative members to ensure that the preparation, handling, and packaging of the food obtained through this Club meet the standards I set forth above. I affirm that no government regulations apply to our products and that regulatory agencies have no jurisdiction over any of our products I obtain through this Club."* In other words, the members of Rawsome accept the risk associated with consuming such foods and believe it is their right to have access to these products. It is difficult for me to understand how this could justify an armed raid.

So far, the fallout from the raid has been minimal. Within hours, Rawsome was back in business, and Stewart had removed the red tag the agents had placed on the cooler to mark its illegality. "In fact, I'm holding it right now," he said when I called him in his apartment. He sounded exceptionally smug. "It's been on my desk for months."

It's hard to know what will come of it all; currently, the club is being pressured by the city's department of building and safety for its lack of permitting, a violation that Stewart readily admits to. However, he's convinced that the real squeeze is coming from the health department, which has realized the limits of its jurisdiction over the club's activities and is therefore pressuring the folks in building and safety to crack down. "They're trying to close us down, because they know the masses are waking up and taking their health in their own hands," said Stewart. "Everybody should have the freedom to put whatever food they want into their body. You know what Hippocrates said: 'Let food be your medicine, and medicine be your food.' It's time to get back to basics."

I'm not going to tell you that I believe everything Aajonus Vonderplanitz and James Stewart say about nutrition, and I'm certainly not going to tell you that eating raw meat is the key to perfect health. There's a roasting chicken in my refrigerator right now, and when I'm finished working for the day, I'm going to go downstairs to the kitchen, crank the oven up to 400°F, and cook that bird until its juices run clear (I love the way the skin crisps up and gets that nice, deep tawny color after it's been in the oven for a couple of hours). So when Aajonus starts talking about eating raw chicken and pork and sucking raw eggs out of their shells, I'm not suggesting you do the same.

But there is one part of this story that I believe we should all take very seriously: the right to eat how we choose, and the right to procure and produce these foods without fear of being raided by pistol-wielding officers of the law. We live in a nation where it is perfectly legal to carry concealed weapons. We are allowed (and, through the medium of advertising, outright encouraged) to purchase products that are undisputedly hazardous to our health: cigarettes, hard alcohol, Big Macs, snack cakes. The cancer sticks alone are estimated to cause 440,000 deaths each year, which means that over the past decade, there have been 4.4 million deaths attributable to smoking. And exactly none attributable to milk intended to be sold unpasteurized. (The CDC attributes two deaths to raw milk over this period, but both were actually from unpasteurized *queso fresco,* a cheese that is consumed almost exclusively by Hispanic communities and produced almost exclusively from raw milk obtained from large-scale dairies where the milk is intended for pasteurization and therefore not held to a particularly high standard of cleanliness.)

To deny people the right to legally purchase the foods they believe are essential to their well-being, no matter how outrageous their beliefs might seem to most Americans, is an insult not only to us but also to the founders of our nation. Could they ever have imagined a day when citizens of the United States would not be able to legally purchase the food of their choosing? And yet, here we are, with armed crackdowns of raw food outlets and almost constant badgering of the farmers who produce unpasteurized milk and other raw dairy products. Fortunately for Aajonus and his followers, we are still allowed access to uncooked meat.

The regulators argue that consumers need to be protected from the failings or simple negligence of producers—in particular, producers supplying products that are pathogen friendly. And to a certain extent, this is true. But it is only true because our food system has become so consolidated and secretive that consumers are no longer afforded the opportunity to make informed choices regarding where they buy their food. Go ahead call any of the major multinational food conglomerates and tell them you'd like to see where your hamburgers are made or where your milk is bottled. The closest you'll get is the parking lot or, if you're really persistent, the lobby. The curtain that hangs between you and where your nourishment originates is thick and dark and doesn't come with draw cords. It is amazing, really: There is no consumer product more essential to your well-being than food, and yet you have *no right* to understand or even see its origins.

Given this distancing, is it really surprising that we can no longer trust our food? Given what we know about corporate culture in 21st-century America, I'd argue that it would be more surprising if we *did* trust our food. And that is a very sad statement on what it means to live in the wealthiest, most "advanced" nation in the world.

11

On an early September morning, I walked with my two young sons downhill through the woods from our northern Vermont home. The morning was warm and promising, the sun punching through the thick forest canopy in scattered bars of soft light. I kept my eyes peeled for the distinctive green shoots of carrot tops, the hoped-for fruit of my springtime seed toss, but alas, I saw none.

I doubt the boys noticed any of this. They were in a state of high agitation, for we carried a container of freshly unearthed worms, a pair of fishing poles, a box of tackle, and the fervent hope that we'd be eating trout for lunch. We were heading for our favorite and almost-secret fishing hole, where the stream that runs along the road below our house widens and deepens to create something of a haven for brook trout. (Well, it *would* be a haven if not for our occasional predatory presence.)

If there is anything my boys love more than eating fish, it is catching them. I have rarely seen them as happy as when they're hauling a wriggling specimen onto the leaf-covered stream bank, where they invariably stoop over it, discussing its various attributes and demerits and comparing it to previous catches. Fishing seems to release qualities both exceeding primal and human, which, if you think about, are pretty much the same things.

This morning did not disappoint. By 9:00 we were heading back up the hill with a pair of slippery speckled brookies. The boys carried their respective catches (I was called upon to haul both poles and tackle) and paused every few steps to admire their bounty. Once, my younger boy tripped over a root in the trail; though he wouldn't admit so, it was because he'd been staring at his catch rather than watching where he placed his feet.

For lunch, we fried the fish in butter and shared them around. Now, brook trout have many traits that make them suitable for lunch, but size is not one of them. Between the two fish, there were perhaps four bites for each of us, including my wife. Four bites of the flaky, slightly sweet flesh. Four bites, each of which required the extraction of multiple tiny bones—little skeletal slivers we lay along the edges of our plates. Of course, fishing is as much about the thrill of the chase as it is the meal that might follow, but I couldn't help thinking: *All of that? For four measly bites? Couldn't something be done?*

As I was about to discover, in the brave new world of 21st-century food production, something very much *can* be done. In fact, the idea that something could be done to make fish grow bigger had long been on the minds of the founders of a Massachusetts-based company called AquaBounty Technologies. To this end, in

2001 AquaBounty filed a New Animal Drug Application (NADA) with the FDA. This was not so unusual; after all, any company that wants to release a veterinary drug in the US market must receive approval from the FDA.

But the fact that a company was filing a NADA application for a fish destined for human consumption provides some context on how our food is changing and how our conversations about food safety need to change with it. The logic behind this process is confusing—*tell me again what an animal drug has to do with the size of fish?*—and it's easy for the layperson to get lost, become frustrated, and give up. Still, it's incredibly important stuff, not just because it is part of our future food landscape, but because it illustrates the profound divide between what we should expect from our regulatory agencies and what we get.

To begin unraveling the story of the animal drug approval process, first you have to understand that the product for which AquaBounty sought (and, as it turns out, still seeks) approval was a genetically engineered (GE) Atlantic salmon that artificially combines growth hormone genes from an unrelated Pacific salmon with DNA from the genes of an eelpout. By manipulating the genes in this fashion, AquaBounty has created a fish—they call it *AquAdvantage*—that produces growth hormone year-round and therefore grows at twice the rate of nonengineered Atlantic salmon. The company's fervent hope is that it will be granted FDA approval for the technology and will be the first business to market genetically engineered animal flesh for human consumption in the United States.

Okay, so you're probably not unconfused quite yet, because if you're like me, you're having a heck of a time following the logic (or lack thereof), which seems to be this: AquaBounty wants to produce a genetically engineered salmon for human consumption, and in order to do so, they need FDA approval. But they don't need FDA approval to produce a particular food; rather, they need the agency's permission to produce a *veterinary drug*? I don't know about you, but when I hold a salmon in one hand and, say, a bottle of cat dewormer in the other, I do not wonder if perhaps the approval process for these two products is the same, because I cannot imagine how it could be. Like I said: logic. *Or lack thereof.*

Turns out, the reasoning behind the FDA's decision to steer the engineered salmon through its NADA process is pretty simple: They didn't know what else to do, because there's no approval process that's specific to genetically engineered animals. The only prior genetically engineered animal to pass muster is an engineered goat that was approved in 2009. But the goat flesh isn't intended for human consumption; rather, the animals are engineered to produce a substance called antithrombin in their milk, for treatment of hereditary antithrombin deficiency, a malady that puts its sufferers at high risk of life-threatening blood clots. In fact, according to the press release that accompanied the FDA's approval of the engineered goats, it was specifically noted that the agency's Center for Veterinary Medicine "made sure that there are adequate procedures in place to prevent the GE goats from entering the food supply." Of course, no such note would accompany the potential approval of AquAdvantage salmon because the fish is being expressly developed for the human food supply.

In any event, and despite the seemingly convoluted trail of reason surrounding the approval process, the FDA was fixing to determine the fate of AquaBounty's salmon right around the same time I took my boys fishing on a certain September morning in 2010, 9 years after the company first filed its application. The process AquaBounty sought approval for looked something like this: The company would ship fertilized eggs to a facility in Panama, where the fish would be raised to market size in dryland confinement facilities high on a mountain before being returned to markets in the United States. The female fish would be sterile, or mostly so: According to data the company submitted to the FDA, up to 5 percent of the fish would remain fertile, raising the specter that genetically engineered escapees could breed with their wild brethren.

To help with their decision, the FDA turned to its Veterinary Medicine Advisory Committee (VMAC), which was standard agency operating procedure for a NADA. But for all its experience, the FDA decided that VMAC didn't have enough specific expertise in the field of genetic engineering, so it convened a panel of four "temporary voting members" to assist with the AquaBounty approval process.

This seemed a reasonable approach; after all, what could be wrong with tapping the expertise of some of the world's finest minds on the subject of the genetic engineering? Nothing, I'd argue, unless said minds had previously demonstrated a specific bias in regards to said technology. So I was more than a little disheartened to learn that of the four "temporary voting members," one was a former Monsanto employee and producer of a pro–genetic engineering video called *Animal*

Biotechnology; another was the project manager and department head of embryology and cell biology at Revivicor, a company that genetically engineers pigs for use in human medicine (for which it will need FDA approval); and yet another authored a paper for the Center for Science in the Public Interest titled "Creating the Proper Environment for Acceptance of Agricultural Biotechnology."

Still, just because the FDA seems to have stacked the deck firmly in AquaBounty's favor doesn't mean the technology is unsafe. After all, AquaBounty says the flesh of their genetically engineered salmon is exactly the same as nonengineered fish. Therefore, they've argued, the product poses no more threat to human health than wild salmon, and FDA approval should be granted. What's more, says AquaBounty, because the fish is exactly the same, there's no need to label it as genetically engineered. I know this because although the company would not grant me an interview, they were happy to e-mail me a canned statement from CEO Ron Stotish. "The flesh if [*sic*] this fish—what the consumer would be eating—is no different from any other North Atlantic Salmon. Since the food is exactly the same then there's no need to label, as a label implies it's different."

Stotish's refusal to speak with me on record rather surprised me, but it probably shouldn't have. He must have recognized that anyone working on a book about food safety and food rights would have some hard questions to ask about both the safety of his product and whether or not his customers should be allowed to know that the fish they were eating was genetically engineered. But if he is really as confident as he claims, why not make himself available for questions? Why not let his answers speak for themselves?

Perhaps because the food-safety implications of AquaBounty's engineered salmon aren't as straightforward as Stotish would have you believe. In fact, it seems that an awful lot of folks are concerned over shortcomings in the FDA's approval process— which, as it turns out, is hugely reliant on studies provided by, well, none other than AquaBounty itself.

But even that isn't what irks Michael Hansen. Rather, Hansen, a senior staff scientist with Consumers Union, the non-profit that publishes *Consumer Reports* magazine, is concerned that the data provided by AquaBounty fails to adequately address the issues at hand. Actually, *concerned* probably isn't the right word, because when I called Hansen (who specializes in genetically modified organisms and genetically engineered food) in his Yonkers, New York, office on the day after he'd returned from the FDA hearings on AquAdvantage salmon, he was in a high-enough state of agitation that *apoplectic* seems more appropriate. "The data is horrendous; it's laughable. That's how bad it is. If an undergraduate tried to write a paper with this data, he would be failed. This is really a piss-poor package."

I felt like saying, *And how do you really feel about the data?* But it seemed a little unprofessional, so I kept my mouth shut and let Hansen continue talking, which, I can assure you, he does with great aplomb.

It would take a book in and of itself to fully address all of Hansen's concerns about AquaBounty's data and the FDA's regulatory process for genetically engineered animals, in large part because the subjects tend to quickly veer into the realm of deep scientific wonkiness that is difficult for the layperson to decipher. Indeed, I had to interrupt Hansen's rapid-fire patter numerous times to request a dumbed-down version of what he'd just said.

First, Hansen is concerned (nay, *apoplectic*) that AquaBounty's test for growth hormone in the flesh of AquAdvantage salmon is not nearly precise enough. Growth hormone in animal flesh is measured in nanograms per gram (a nanogram is one billionth of a gram). According to Hansen, AquaBounty measured growth hormone levels in 73 fish and found measurable amounts in exactly none.

Well, that sounds pretty good, right? Not really, says Hansen, because the limit of detection for the company's monitoring equipment was 10.4 nanograms per gram. "I can show you studies where the level in wild salmon is 1 nanogram per gram, and they're using 10.4 as a baseline?" He voice was pitched high with incredulity. "It's like using a radar gun that doesn't detect speeds below 120 mph and concluding that cars and bikes don't move at different speeds."

The issue of growth hormone in the flesh of the fish isn't the only thing that concerns Hansen (although, considering that the particular hormone we're talking about—IGF-1—has been associated with increased risk of a number of cancers, including prostate, breast, colorectal, and lung, he has plenty to lose sleep over). At various points in our conversation, he called the data on potential allergenicity "weak," "poor," and "sloppy." "They basically blew that one off," he said, sounding nothing less than disgusted.

Michael Hansen seemed so irritated—almost enraged—by the data and the general lack of rigor in the regulatory process for GE animals destined for human consumption that I began to wonder if perhaps he had a personal or professional ax to grind. So I called Jaydee Hanson (no relation; note the different spelling of their surnames). Hanson is the director for human genetics policy for the Institute on Biotechnology and the Human Future as well as policy analyst on cloning and genetics for the nongovernmental Center for Food Safety, where he specializes in issues relating to animal cloning and animal genetic engineering. The guy must have a hell of a big business card.

The Hanson with an *o* differs from the one with an *e* in that he speaks at perhaps half the speed and seemed less angry rather than simply bewildered. "One of the ways the FDA decides whether animals are safe to eat is to look at whether they're healthy," he explained. "The health of the animals is used by the FDA as explicit proxy." That makes sense: If an animal is sick, do you really want to eat it?

According to Hanson, there are valid questions surrounding the health of the engineered salmon. "They have a higher degree of skeletal malformations, which is probably not surprising, since they grow twice as fast. They have more jaw erosion, and enlarged gills, and there is focal inflammation in the flesh; basically, they have arthritis of the flesh. Now, none of this means that this animal is definitively not safe to eat, but it sure does raise some red flags."

I pointed out that the health of livestock does not always seem a priority to the FDA: Witness the sorry condition of cattle, chickens, and pigs reared in CAFOs. True, noted Hanson, but "it's easier with cows, because cows that can't walk through the gate to the slaughterhouse aren't supposed to be killed. There's no gate that fish have to swim through."

Both Hansen and Hanson were somewhat encouraged by the fact that the FDA's advisory panel—as biotech friendly as it appeared to be—seemed to share many of their concerns. "The legal standard is 'Do the data demonstrate reasonable certainty of no harm?'" Michael Hansen told me. "Nobody at the hearing said 'yes' to that, including the FDA's own advisory panel."

But the FDA is not required to follow the advice of its own advisory panel. Or, even if they do, they could approve the engineered fish *and* ask for further research, which would basically shift the burden of risk to the general public. Neither Hansen nor Hanson was willing to make specific predictions regarding the chances of approval for AquAdvantage salmon, but both believe that the approval of genetically engineered meat for human consumption is a matter of "when," not "if." "I think the FDA staff, many of whom used to work for the biotech industry, is so committed to approving these animals that they'll be approved," said Hanson. "In my opinion, the FDA basically thinks these things are okay and wants to move them through."

If true (and frankly, even if not), this is more than a little alarming, because it seems altogether clear that the approval process currently in place at the FDA does not adequately address the unique issues of genetically engineered meat destined for human consumption. The FDA would like us to be reassured that they've applied as much rigor as they have; after all, the AquAdvantage salmon could have been pushed through without a public comment period, rather than the 14 days provided. "We do look at this very, very carefully," FDA spokesperson Siobhan DeLancey told me. "And we really feel that that the New Animal Drug approval process satisfies the evaluation needs quite well. You don't necessarily need new regulations to adapt product to process."

DeLancey was similarly enthusiastic about the transparency of the GE salmon approval process. "The public saw all of the data. That's unprecedented." It is also an exaggeration. What the public was allowed to see (and DeLancey admitted this when I asked) were FDA summaries of the data that were *provided by the very company seeking approval*. What's that saying? I'm pretty sure it's not "the devil is in the summaries."

DeLancey didn't sound like an arrogant person, but I was struck by the arrogance in her contention (which, in her defense, is almost certainly a company line she's simply repeating) that the process should take precedence over the product. It is all but an outright admission that the FDA simply doesn't have the proper procedures in place to deal with emerging food technologies like GE salmon.

Michael Hansen agrees. "What we have is a patchwork that doesn't apply. They're trying to fit square pegs into round holes. The fact that they're treating this as a drug shows you how unprepared they are to deal with this sort of technology."

Some people believe it's a bit less innocent than that. Mansour Samadpour, the president of IEH Laboratories in Seattle, who made an appearance during our discussion about pathogenic *E. coli,* takes a slightly more jaundiced view. "It is extremely hard for regulatory agencies to make new rules," he told me

But not in Enviropig, which produces an enzyme in its salivary glands that allows it render the phytic acid digestible. This increases the feed efficiency of the engineered pig as well as reduces the phosphorus in its excretions by up to 60 percent.

All of which sounds well and good, but given the approval process for AquAdvantage salmon, I am not confident that the FDA is prepared for the unique risks associated with genetically engineered animals destined for human consumption, no matter how much phosphorus they have in their feces. Indeed, I am not confident that the FDA even knows what the risks are or, if it does, cares enough to address them. And this dearth of confidence can lead me to only one conclusion: I don't want this stuff on the market. In this I am not alone: A poll conducted by Lake Research Partners in September 2010 showed that 91 percent of those surveyed feel the FDA should not allow genetically engineered fish and meat into the marketplace without further research. Ninety-one percent.

The approval process for AquAdvantage (and, unless an awful lot changes in the near future, for Enviropig), with all its bad and incomplete science and omitted details, does tremendous damage to our national psyche pertaining to food: It undermines the credibility of the FDA (and by extension, the other agencies associated with food safety) and erodes the trust of the public it is assigned to protect. In the current climate of extreme unease regarding the safety of our food, this is particularly dangerous. If consumers feel as though they can't trust the providers of their nourishment, and at the same time feel they can't trust the regulatory agencies that are supposed to serve as the primary line of defense against unscrupulous producers . . . well, then, who can they trust?

Again, I find myself considering how the issue of morality infuses almost every aspect of our food industry and our relationship with it. Of course, the same could probably be said of any industry, and yet it seems to me that there is a special burden—if you want to call it that—to be borne by the producers and regulators of our nourishment. This is, after all, the most essential commerce we engage in, and we engage in it every day of our lives. This is about what we put into our bodies to keep us alive. To wonder if perhaps food safety should be treated with an exceptional level of respect and perhaps even reverence does not seem like too much to ask.

12

As it turned out, during the time I was writing this book I would have the opportunity to witness firsthand and in real time one of the largest foodborne illness outbreaks and subsequent food recalls in the history of humankind. The drama began to unfold on August 13, 2010, when Wright County Egg initiated a voluntary nationwide recall of shell eggs due to *Salmonella* Enteritidis contamination at three of its five farms. Within a week, the recall would twice be expanded to include eggs from a second producer that shared suppliers with Wright County Egg. Soon the total number of eggs recalled exceeded more than a half billion (yes, half a *billion*) being sold under no fewer than 16 brand names. That's 550 million eggs, 16 brands, 14 US states, and 1,800 people sickened. *From two suppliers.* If those numbers don't tell a tale of an industry run amuck, I'm not sure what does.

Over the past 2 decades, *Salmonella* Enteritidis has become the single most common cause of foodborne illness in the United States. It is one of the three strains of *Salmonella enterica* that account for nearly half the deaths by foodborne pathogenic bacteria in this country: *Salmonella* Typhi, *Salmonella* Typhimurium, and *Salmonella* Enteritidis. *S.* Typhi is the bacterium that causes typhoid fever; it is typically spread by contaminated water (although food that's been washed in contaminated water can also be a vector). Owing to the generally high quality of North America's water supply, *S.* Typhi is not very common.

Next up is *S.* Typhimurium, which in mice causes a typhoidlike disease. In humans, it does not cause as severe a reaction as *S.* Typhi, and it is not normally fatal, although the severe diarrhea, abdominal cramps, and vomiting that accompany it are not anybody's idea of a picnic. And in people with compromised or undeveloped immune systems (the young, elderly, or those fighting other serious conditions, such as cancer), *S.* Typhimurium can be a death sentence, particularly if it's not quickly identified and treated with antibiotics.

Which brings us to the culprit of the big egg outbreak of 2010, *S.* Enteritidis, which inflicts symptoms that are for all intents and purposes indistinguishable from *S.* Typhimurium. (At a DNA level, the three strains of *S. enterica* are 95 to 99 percent identical and, it surprised me to learn, share about 65 percent of their DNA with *E. coli*.) The thing about *S.* Enteritidis is that it is extremely prevalent in chicken flocks, where it can thrive and spread undetected. Indeed, many people believe that the rise of *S.* Enteritidis in the United States has everything to do with the consolidation of the chicken industry (both for eggs and meat) over the past few decades. It is estimated that *S.* Enteritidis causes as many as 140,000 human illnesses annually.

The moment I heard about the egg recall, I couldn't help thinking of Bill Marler (much to my regret, I also couldn't quite shake the image—and the sound—of Aajonus Vonderplanitz slurping a raw egg from its shell). I imagined Marler in his glass-walled office high in the Seattle skyline, passing the handful of minutes between phone calls from claimants and reporters, and coming up with withering quips aimed at the egg industry and our regulatory agencies. Turns out, I wasn't too far off: On August 17, only 4 days after the recall was announced, Marler Clark announced that it had filed its first lawsuit associated with the outbreak. And on August 23, CNBC included this Marlerism in its "quotations of the day": *"The history of ignoring the law makes the sickening of 1,300 and the forced recall of 550 million eggs shockingly understandable. You have to wonder where the USDA and FDA inspectors were."* I had to smile; the quip was classic Marler, and it appeared between quotes from General Ray Odierno and Iranian President Mahmoud Ahmadinejad. I could only imagine how much Marler would like that.

To be honest, I hadn't paid much attention during the early days of the outbreak; part of this was simply because, like most Americans, I'd become accustomed to news of foodborne illness and, therefore, somewhat inured to its impact. It was like hearing about yet another traffic accident on the nightly news: *Oh, another outbreak. That's too bad.* Part of it was because, like Bill Marler, I knew something about the legal, regulatory, and sanitary conditions surrounding our modern food industry and the ways in which they conjoin to all but ensure that such outbreaks are, as Marler himself put it, "shockingly understandable." And part of it, I'll admit, was because we keep a small flock of laying hens on our Vermont farm. I hadn't bought a grocery store egg in at least a decade, and I sure as heck wasn't about to begin now.

But as the outbreak grew, I began to focus my attention. And as I focused, I began to realize that the egg-related salmonella outbreak of August 2010 was an almost perfect summation of the risks inherent to our consolidated, corporatized food system, a system that has become so entrenched and pervasive that such incidents hardly raise eyebrows among anyone familiar with the way the business of our nourishment is conducted.

Wright County Egg is located in Galt, Iowa, a north-central Iowa town with a population of just 30 (no, I am not forgetting any zeros). This means that there are approximately 14,999,970 more chickens than people residing in Galt, which seems like a perilous imbalance: I mean, chickens are pretty docile creatures, but if ever they got in the mood to revolt, the good people of Galt would have a hell of a fight on their hands.

The business is owned by Austin "Jack" DeCoster, who also owns Quality Egg, the company that supplies young chickens (known as pullets) and feed to both Wright County Egg and Hillandale Farms. That's pretty much par for the course, as most of the large-scale egg and meat production in modern agriculture operates under the "vertical integration" model. Vertical integration is just a fancy way of saying that a common owner controls numerous businesses necessary to complete a particular supply chain: the feed that feeds the layers, the chicks that become laying hens, the laying hens and the eggs they supply.

Which came first, the chicken or the egg? If anyone knows, it's Jack DeCoster, because his hands are in every piece of the process; it all falls under his purview.

As the outbreak dragged on and various media outlets began digging, it became clear that Jack DeCoster knows a few other things, too. In particular, he knows how to pay fines and settlements, including $3.6 million to the Occupational Safety and Health Administration in 1996, for violations in the workplace and at workers' housing (then–Secretary of Labor Robert B. Reich publicly denounced DeCoster's practices as "morally repugnant" and "among the worst we found around the country." At the time, DeCoster's egg empire was located in rural Maine.

Even as he was being fined for these abuses, DeCoster was expanding his empire into Iowa, where he established a sprawling hog business that included a half-dozen facilities scattered throughout north-central Iowa. Like most industrial-scale livestock producers, DeCoster wisely chooses to locate his businesses far beyond the watchful eyes, sensitive noses, and political sway of urban population centers. Almost immediately, he was fined $59,000 for numerous water pollution and animal waste control violations. Shortly thereafter, the Iowa attorney general came knocking, bestowing upon DeCoster the dubious distinction of being the state's first habitual offender of water quality laws. That title cost him $150,000. Then in 2002, Wright County Eggs paid $1.5 million to settle a lawsuit filed by five illegal Mexican immigrants who claimed they were raped by supervisors who threatened to have them fired or killed if they didn't submit to their advances.

Of course, one could argue that none of this speaks directly to the issue of salmonella in eggs or that this pattern of behavior—however distasteful—is not confined to our food industry. Both arguments are strictly true, but DeCoster's sordid history tells a larger truth about the practice of agriculture in 21st-century America, and it is this: There is a sad lack of reverence in the business of the most life-giving commerce we know. One would like to think that the production of food would carry with it a sense of responsibility to conduct oneself and one's business in a manner befitting the critical importance of the end product, and that this ethos would resonate throughout the industry. But one would be wrong, and the reason for this is that we have come to view food as simply another fungible commodity. An egg is an egg is an egg, which isn't really even an egg, but rather a nutritional unit to be plugged into an engineered dietary formulation. Which will probably be changed next year, according to the latest fad or study refuting its validity. Given this coldly calculating view of our nourishment, is it any surprise that we've come to treat our food as little more than an economic sector, in which success or failure relates more to food's ability to feed our economy than to nourish our bodies and minds.

The 2010 egg outbreak was also notable for the technology that was used to track it: pulsed-field gel electrophoresis (PFGE). In fact, the CDC had been on alert since May, when the agency noticed a marked uptick in the number of *Salmonella* Enteritidis isolates with PFGE pattern JEGX01.0004 (the bacterium's DNA fingerprint) being uploaded to the PulseNet database. Between May 1 and July 31, a total of 1,953 illnesses were reported; this was nearly three times what the

CDC considers "normal" for the time frame (typically, there would have been about 700 salmonella cases reported). Of course, not all of these illnesses were egg related, but it was clear to the government that something big was brewing.

This is, in essence, how modern foodborne-illness investigations are conducted in the early years of the 21st century, and it is in many regards a textbook example of an investigation done right: Technology was utilized to identify an outbreak and focus the investigation, and epidemiologists were deployed to pinpoint the guilty food and where that food originated. The producer recalled the offending food, and the public was alerted to avoid eggs from these suppliers.

Except: Why did it take almost 4 months between the first spike on PulseNet and the initial recall? The CDC's own data show a clear rise beginning in the middle of April; it's not terribly dramatic, but it's there. Given the modest nature of the initial rise in cases, it seems reasonable that they would wait a week or two for confirmation. After all, perhaps the increase was simple coincidental; maybe the number of cases would fall to historical norms over the next few weeks.

It didn't. Instead, it spiked dramatically in the final week of April and first weeks of May. Any hope that this might be simply a bad month or a statistical aberration was blown right out of the water. Studying the chart released by the CDC, it seems painfully clear that something was amiss as early as the first of May. Which means it took $3\frac{1}{2}$ months from the time the CDC had to have known there was a problem to the initial recall of eggs on August 13. I don't know about you, but in my view this is not the sort of time gap that engenders confidence.

BEN HEWITT

If the CDC and FDA truly need the better part of 100 days to make a connection between a spike in illnesses relating to a common foodborne pathogen and the actual food associated with the outbreak, might we be looking at a more systemic problem? Could it be that a supply chain in which two producers sell eggs under more than a dozen brands in numerous states throughout the United States is inherently unsafe? Consider: During the 100 days it took epidemiologists to trace the pathogen to its source, using the latest gee-whiz technology and the full resources of two of our nation's largest, best-funded agencies, more than 1,000 people got sick.

Still, I couldn't understand why it had taken so long to find the source of the outbreak. I was suspicious that perhaps the CDC and FDA had known exactly where the salmonella was coming from for days, if not weeks, prior to the initial recall. Remember: These agencies don't have the authority to shut down a facility or even force a recall. All they can do is alert a producer to a problem and suggest a response.

So I called Marler, whose 15 minutes of fame had stretched to at least 3 weeks and included an appearance on *Larry King Live* as well as daily news programs on CNN and MSNBC. He'd been withering in his criticism of both the producers and the government.

Maybe he was simply feeling mellow, or perhaps his run of media appearances had worn him out ("I think people are getting overwhelmed by Marler on TV, and I can't blame them," he told me), but Marler was more circumspect and empathetic toward the federal agencies than I'd expected. "You've got the local health guys saying, 'Don't blame me, blame the state.' And

212

the state says, 'Don't blame me, blame the CDC.' And the CDC says, 'We can't do anything if we don't have good information from the local guys.'"

What about my theory—which, to be fair, wasn't strictly mine; I'd seen it posited by numerous observers—that the contamination source point had been known for some time and the recall had been delayed by ongoing negotiations over the response? Almost certainly not true, Marler told me. "My guess is that probably around the 10th of August, the CDC felt it had enough data to call Wright County Egg and say, 'You guys have a big f'ing problem.' This whole issue of mandatory recall is a red herring." For one thing, he explained, there's not much practical difference between the government asking for a recall and mandating a recall; to say "no" would invite an uncomfortable level of scrutiny and pressure. Also, the negative publicity generated by refusing to recall a product linked to hundreds, if not thousands, of illnesses would likely be a producer's death knell. Better to absorb the temporary, if severe, economic pain doled out by a recall and carry on.

The reason for the long lag between the observed spike in salmonella cases and the recall, explained Marler, isn't one of "mal-intent" or simple laziness. No, it's more systemic than that, a result of our nation's disjointed efforts when it comes to recognizing and tracking outbreaks of foodborne illness and their source points. He trotted out his funnel analogy again (by this point I'd heard it at least three times, but it still struck me as apt): Because the CDC can only know about the cases that emerge from the narrow end of the funnel, and because so much occurs inside the funnel to obfuscate the situation, and because the narrow and fat ends of the funnel are often separated by thousands of miles, it can take quite a while to determine where any particular outbreak originated.

I'd assumed that Marler would be inundated with calls from claimants and wannabe claimants who had become ill (or believed they had become ill) by eating contaminated eggs. But as it turns out, the phones had been relatively quiet, and Marler was pretty sure he knew why. "When outbreaks take several months to figure out, stuff falls through the cracks." Remember, the first spike in salmonella cases happened in late April and early May, but it wasn't until the middle of August that these incidents could be connected to a particular food and producer. In other words, nearly 4 months passed between the first cases and the identification of a defendant on which to lay blame. *Salmonella* Enteritidis isn't a particularly pleasant affliction. (Hint: You'll get real familiar with the business end of your bathroom.) But it's rarely serious and even more rarely fatal. In other words, people get sick from it, recover, and move on. Even in litigation-happy America, suing over a tummy ache hasn't become standard practice.

There are two ways to view the story of the great egg outbreak of 2010: as the story of a pathogen and the effort to halt its spread. Or as the story of an industry that, like virtually every segment of our food system, prizes scale and efficiency above all else, because scale and efficiency equal profit, even as they drive the price of our nourishment to historic lows. The business of producing eggs in this country has changed—and changed recently and rapidly—in ways that are mirrored throughout the food industry. According to Iowa State University's Agricultural Marketing Resource Center, in 1987 there were 2,500 egg producers with at least 75,000 hens. Today, the number of producers operating on such a scale has dropped to 205, and that's not because over the past 25 years thousands of small-scale producers have entered the market. Rather, it's exactly the opposite: The biggest egg farms have gotten exponentially bigger, and in 2010, the 205 largest farms produce 95 percent of the eggs that make their way to American tables.

What is the reward for such consolidation? If you are Jack DeCoster, it is measured in growth and profit; if you're an egg consumer, it is the low price attached to each of those fragile, oblong orbs, which as of January 2010 averaged less than 12 cents apiece. At first blush, this arrangement sounds okay: Let DeCoster have his profit; give us our cheap eggs. Except we get something more than cheap eggs: We get a system that's capable of spreading pathogenic bacteria just as easily as it spreads 12-penny eggs.

Something else strikes me about the great egg outbreak of 2010, and it is the absolute clarity with which the situation illustrates our government's priorities when "protecting" us from our food. On June 30, 2010, even as national salmonella cases were spiking more than 400 percent higher than normal, California state agents were raiding the warehouse at Rawsome with their guns drawn. How many cases of illness were associated with the Rawsome food-buying club? Well, none actually. Not one, not two or even three. Certainly not 1,800, which would be the final tally of illness linked to the egg outbreak.

On one hand, we have one of the largest foodborne-illness outbreaks in the United States, perpetrated by a consolidated industry that can't even be legally compelled to recall its product in the face of irrefutable evidence of contamination. We have a company run by a man with numerous violations in his recent history, Iowa's first "habitual offender," but who is nonetheless allowed to continue expanding his agricultural enterprise. We have an industry that, like most food-based industries, conducts its business entirely out of sight of its customers; as of July 2010, it is actually *illegal* for egg farms with more than 3,000 hens to allow the public into the chicken houses. The stated reason for this is that visitors can carry pathogenic bacteria on their clothing or shoes, which is almost funny, given what the FDA found in the laying houses at Wright County Egg: piles of chicken manure as high as 8 feet; rodents and wild birds, both common vectors of pathogenic bacteria; and dead flies "too numerous to count."

On the other hand, we have a buying club of approximately 1,600 members who willingly consume foods the FDA and USDA believe to be dangerous. We have an establishment that sources its foods from farmers who welcome visits by those who consume their products. We have no reported illness. We have consumers who trust their food and are willing to pay a premium for it precisely because they feel as if they can trust it.

I am not making claims about the safety and health benefits of raw foods; I'll leave that to Mark McAfee and Aajonus Vonderplanitz. I am only pointing out the absurdity of our nation's food-safety-related laws and regulations. When an outfit like Rawsome, with zero history of foodborne illness and the willing participation of its members, can be shut down by gun-toting agents, while businesses like Wright County Egg and Hillandale Farms can't even be legally compelled to cease operations after they make 1,800 people ill and force the recall of more than half a billion eggs, there can be little doubt where our government's priorities lie.

We have learned (or been taught) to consider the issue of food safety only in the context of a system that is inherently unsafe, that wields both economic might and political power. Part of this, I think, is that we have only begun to think seriously about food safety in the past few decades, a time frame that is concurrent with the rise of industrial agriculture and food corporatism and concurrent with a sense that we are utterly beholden to this system. And to a certain extent, we are: Most of us have become displaced from the land and disconnected from the source of our nourishment.

And yet we must eat. So we place a shaky trust in the producers who time and again betray us and in a government that seems powerless to truly protect us. Outbreak after outbreak, we return to the same supermarkets to buy the same food from the same system that has proven itself incapable of cleaning up its act and that is feeding us products that, if they don't make us acutely ill, sicken us over the course of years and decades. *Because we think we have no choice.*

Given this sense of helplessness, is it any wonder that our collective responses to the inherent vulnerabilities of such a system are in large part framed by the system itself? We seem unable to consider another way, even as it becomes more obvious that we must. We barely question the wisdom of having two producers supplying the eggs for 16 brands in nearly half the United States. We don't pause to wonder if perhaps an inexpensive egg is also a cheap egg, or how the ways in which our desire for ever-cheaper food butts up against the need for food corporations to make money. This is not to absolve Wright County Egg or Hillandale Farms of their egregious violations, but it is a fact that the current model of food production in this country lacks both transparency and accountability, even as it seeks to profit in an industry with notoriously tight margins. Of course corners will be cut; thus it has always been, thus it always will be.

By comparing the Rawsome raid to the egg recall, I'm not trying to make a claim about a specific food and its relative safety. Oh sure, I have my opinions, and given the choice, I'll take my chances with the illegal goods at Rawsome rather than risk my well-being by eating an egg from a so-called "farm" where the chickens live in cages amid piles of excrement and in the company of rodents.

But that's not the point. Or rather, it's not the point I'm trying to make right now. Rather, what I hope this comparison makes clear is the ways in which our government's response to outbreaks of foodborne illness is built on faulty assumptions. First, there is an assumption that consumers should not be allowed or do not care to view how their food is raised. Second, there is an assumption that certain foods—such as the ones available at Rawsome— are more dangerous or at least more deserving of heavy-handed oversight than the eggs emerging from a 15-million-hen "farm." Third, there is the assumption that the level of consolidation from which a half-billion-egg recall arises is a healthy business model. Perhaps most alarmingly, there is an assumption that individuals should not have the right to make informed choices about the food they consume.

Is it ironic that all of these assumptions and the responses to them merely propagate the systemic weaknesses of our food system? Is it ironic that in a country where tobacco is sold in every corner store and the right to bear arms is written into the constitution, we have no right to specific foods? The people who eat from Rawsome *want* that food. None of them are complaining about foodborne illness. The farms that supply the store are small in scale and located in the region; if there were an outbreak, it would affect relatively few people and be relatively easy to trace to its source. Having not visited them, I can't comment on the actual practices of these farms, but given the legal framework of the business, in which the consumers are leasing the properties, it's unlikely they would be denied access to the source of their food should they seek it out. In other words, there is built-in transparency. There is built-in accountability. As Bill Marler quipped when I visited him in Seattle: "Just because you can shake the hand of the farmer who sold you your dinner doesn't mean he's not going to poison you. But it does mean you'll know where to find him if he does."

Yet the regulatory landscape in this country places a business like Rawsome directly in the crosshairs of our agriculture and food-related agencies, even as it enables a business like Wright County Egg to operate with a past and present of flagrant violations. Even as it allows the food system in our nation to spiral further out of control, consolidating both the power and practice of agriculture and production, all but ensuring that outbreaks of foodborne illness will only increase in scope and frequency. Even as the final frayed strands of our trust and health are broken.

13

We have come this far without having examined the current structure of incentives surrounding America's agricultural system. The ways in which we encourage the production of certain foods (but not others) via payments to farmers might seem somewhat disconnected from the issue of food safety, but as I'm about to argue, it has led to exponentially more pain, suffering, and even death than all strains of pathogenic bacteria combined. Indeed, if we are ever to realize a truly comprehensive definition of "safe food," it is essential that we understand how our nation's ag-related policies have led to sweeping changes in the businesses of food production, processing, distribution, and even eating. The last in this list might, at first glance, seem unrelated to the agricultural policies implemented by our government, but as you'll see, it is very much connected in ways that might surprise you.

First, let us briefly examine the chief agency responsible for disseminating the subsidies that have played a massive role in shaping the American food landscape and, in the process, the actual American landscape. The United States Department of Agriculture is perhaps the best known of our food and ag-related agencies and, befitting its place at the top of the heap, has its hands in numerous facets of agriculture and its byproducts, along with a few other things you probably weren't aware of. The USDA's annual budget totals $149 billion for 2011, which I think you'll agree is a nice little chunk of change. That reflects a rather substantial increase over the past few years: In 2008, the budget was a "mere" $93 billion. To put the USDA budget in context, consider that the Department of Homeland Security chews up about $55 billion annually, while the Department of Defense is good for more than $700 billion.

The USDA does a lot of things with its loot; as I skimmed through its 157-page 2011 budget report, I was frankly stunned by the depth and reach of the agency into facets of American and even global life that I'd never considered. The United States is a major exporter of agricultural products, totaling nearly $80 billion annually, and agriculture accounts for 1.2 percent of the US gross domestic product. So I suppose it only makes sense that one of the strategic goals laid out in the agency's budget is to "help America promote agricultural production and biotechnology exports as America works to increase food security." In other words, help us sell more food and, in particular, food that is derived from new technologies, including genetic engineering. That's not me twisting the USDA's words, by the way. Under the "key efforts" heading, the number-two goal is to "enhance America's ability to develop and trade agricultural products derived from new technologies." If I were in the business of big ag, I'd really appreciate that effort.

Cynicism aside, the USDA does some good work with our money. For one, it oversees the Special Supplemental Nutrition Program for Women, Infants, and Children (WIC Program) and provides soil and water conservation technical assistance for farmers and property owners. For 2011, it is requesting $30 million for its Sustainable Agriculture Research and Education program, which provides competitive grants to scientists and producers experimenting with sustainable farming techniques.

Particular to the issues of foodborne illness that fall under its purview, the USDA oversees the Food Safety and Inspection Service, a $1 billion program that, according to the mission statement on its Web site, "is the public health agency in the US Department of Agriculture responsible for ensuring that the nation's commercial supply of meat, poultry, and egg products is safe, wholesome, and correctly labeled and packaged." (FSIS is also the agency that Bill Marler suggested to me should mandate the tattooing of its mission statement on every employee's body. Presumably somewhere they will see it frequently.)

The USDA does something else with our money that arguably has more impact on the health and well-being of Americans than all its other programs combined. (Notice how I keep calling it "our money?" Well, that's because it is; we are talking about a taxpayer-funded agency, after all.) The USDA hands out billions of dollars' worth of agricultural subsidies each and every year, part of the farm income stabilization portion of the US farm bill, a 5-year ag-policy bill that was passed into law on June 18, 2008 (the first US farm bill began in 1965 as a multi-year bill, and a revised version has been passed approximately every 5 years since). Most of these dollars are earmarked for farmers cultivating America's five most prolific crops: corn, cotton, rice, wheat, and soybeans.

In 2009, for example, growers of these five crops pulled in $15.4 billion, while growers of "specialty crops," which include fruits, nuts, and vegetables, received a mere $825 million.

As if that imbalance weren't pernicious enough, consider that agricultural subsidies disproportionately benefit a tiny number of large-scale operations, a fact that stands in contrast to the popular myth that subsidies exist to keep small farms afloat. In fact, fully 60 percent of American farmers don't receive any subsidies at all; of the remaining 40 percent, 10 percent receive nearly three-quarters of the cash that's handed out. This has helped create an emerging generation of megafarms. In 1982, farms with at least $1 million in sales accounted for 25 percent of US agricultural output; today, they are responsible for over half.

Making sense of American agricultural subsidies in the early part of the 21st century is a daunting task, in part because they are both complex and convoluted and in part because they simply don't seem to make much sense at all. "The US agricultural subsidy program is a labyrinth," Don Carr told me when I called him at the Environmental Working Group, a nonprofit that monitors and tracks subsidy payouts. "There are people who spend their careers studying the program and can still barely keep up with it."

As Carr explains it, more than 20 programs fall under the rubric of "commodity subsidies." They range from the $5 billion annually in direct payments, which are not based on need and are paid to farmers regardless of market conditions or other factors; to the Conservation Reserve Program, under which our current secretary of agriculture, Tom Vilsack, collected $62,805 over the past decade; to the Crop Insurance Program, whereby the USDA foots 50 percent of the premium for catastrophic coverage. The Conservation Reserve Program, by the way, is intended to help landowners address natural resource conservation issues, such as soil erosion or water quality.

It was not always this complicated (and it is currently much more so than what I've just described). Ag subsidies as we currently know and define them were enacted in the years following World War I, when commodity prices collapsed on the global market. This was a direct response to Europe's war-diminished economy, which could no longer afford to import massive quantities of food from the United States. Like most commodity crashes, it came on the heels of a production bubble: American farmers had recently expanded to meet the needs of hungry Allied forces, utilizing the rapidly evolving agricultural technology of the day to churn out more food than ever. Land that had been grazed by animals since the days of abundant buffalo populations was quickly converted to grain production to cash in on the boom.

Things might've worked out okay, at least in the short term, if not for the drought that followed directly on the heels of this unprecedented expansion of American crop-growing acreage. In the southwestern United States, in a region commonly known as the "Staked Plains," cultivated acreage more than tripled between 1925 and 1930, and this sort of increase was common throughout our nation's breadbasket. Native prairie grasses were plowed under, leaving the fragile topsoil exposed and vulnerable. What little rain did fall quickly evaporated in the hot midwestern sun, and when the winds blew, countless particles of dust were carried aloft. The Dust Bowl had begun.

As if it weren't enough that American farmers had just lost a significant chunk of their global business and were now being chased off the farm by the endless dust storms, the Great Depression was establishing its crushing grip. Suddenly, millions of Americans couldn't afford food basics, and farmers found themselves sitting on massive piles of grain they couldn't sell even as their fellow countrymen and women went hungry. To put it mildly, it was not a good time to be farming in America.

So the government stepped in. This would not be the first time the US government came to the aid of its farmers (remember the government-run seed program?), but it marked a dramatic shift in American agricultural policy. Previous efforts, such as the Homestead Act, had all been aimed at developing the infrastructure and providing the inputs necessary to enable growth and success. But now, having done that job all too well, the country was faced with an entirely different problem: how to support an industry that had grown too big, too fast, and was now floundering in the face of many and varied forces.

Thus came the aptly named Agricultural Adjustment Act of 1933, a nifty little piece of New Deal legislation that paid farmers to reduce production in hopes of bringing some equilibrium in the demand-supply equation. In other words, it had just become law to pay farmers not only for what they grew but also for what they *didn't* grow, which sounds like pretty nice work if you can get it.

That's a bit flip, of course: The producers who were getting paid to allow their fields to lie fallow weren't exactly laughing all the way to the bank. Since 1929, farm income had fallen by over 50 percent, and the nation was mired in the Great Depression. Many farmers were suffering under the oppressive clouds of dust and relentless drought that characterized the Dust Bowl; the implementation of the Agricultural Adjustment Act didn't exactly mark a U-turn in their fortunes.

But it did unquestionably mark the dawn of a new agricultural era in the United States, one whereby the rules that had forever dictated the farm market—supply, demand, weather, disease, and so on—were manipulated and forced to cede to federal oversight. For the next 40 or so years, US farm policy spun on an axis of "supply management" that attempted (and at least partially succeeded) to smooth over the boom and bust cycles inherent to commodity markets—and in particular, commodity markets that are affected by forces beyond human control. Over this period, American farm policy was relatively equitable, offering a degree of stability to large-scale and family farmers alike.

That did not last, and the reason it did not last can be summed up in one name: Earl Butz. One can only imagine the childhood cruelty aimed at a boy named Butz, but Earl wasn't about to let the bullies get him down. Instead, he applied himself to the business of agriculture, first on his parent's 160-acre

Indiana farm, then in a variety of ag-related associations, before serving as assistant secretary of agriculture in the Eisenhower administration and becoming dean of agriculture at Purdue University. But it wasn't until 1971 when President Nixon appointed him secretary of agriculture that Butz began to shape the American diet.

The way he did this was disarmingly simple: Rather than attempt to balance supply and demand via the lever of government policy, typically by encouraging supply restrictions, Butz did everything he could to promote what he called "fence row to fence row" farming. Dissenters worried that the scheme would result in massive surpluses and a subsequent price collapse, but Butz insisted that global markets and a growing population would absorb surplus production, thereby avoiding the bust component of previous boom and bust cycles.

Just as conditions of the late 1920s and early 1930s had converged to give rise to the original ag-subsidy program, the early '70s saw a chain of events that made Butz look like a prophetic genius. In 1972, Russia suffered an abysmal grain harvest; to meet demand, they turned to the United States, where they were able to purchase two-thirds of America's wheat reserves at a bargain price. (In order to ensure a favorable price, Russia had concealed the truly desperate nature of its crop failure. The deal would come to be known as the Great Grain Robbery.) Thus Butz's assertion that international markets would buy up America's grain surplus was proved—at least for one season—correct.

On the heels of the Russian deal, US food commodity prices went ballistic. Farmers were soon enjoying tremendous profits, and Earl Butz's standing rose exponentially. But before long, something else began rising: domestic food prices. Sitting in the political hot seat, Nixon commanded Butz to orchestrate an immediate increase in grain production. Butz, who must have felt as if he'd just been handed the keys to America's agricultural kingdom, used his newly minted credibility with the nation's farm industry to make good on Nixon's order. Thus began the era of never-ending American agricultural plenty.

What does any of this have to do with food safety, you may ask? Imagine a farm industry that is suddenly being encouraged to produce more grain (yes, corn is a grain) than ever before, more grain, in fact, than food producers know what to do with. After all, of $113.6 billion in taxpayer-paid commodity subsidies doled out by the USDA between 1995 and 2004, $41.8 billion went to corn growers. That's more than cotton, soy, and rice combined.

No wonder that corn has become the poster grain of America's agricultural industry; no wonder that, with subsidies flowing like corn kernels through a grain chute, this abundance quickly becomes the new normal. No wonder that the never-ending flow of commodity food ingredients dragged prices steadily lower, thereby encouraging food producers to dream up ways to utilize these bargain inputs. And no wonder that the primary building block of these new foodlike products is corn—most frequently, corn that has been engineered into high fructose corn syrup (HFCS). The result: Between the early 1970s and 2008, annual US consumption of HFCS per capita rose from practically nothing (to be fair, it wasn't invented until 1971) to 38 pounds.

Finally, consider this: In 1971, when Earl Butz took command of US agricultural policy, the obesity rate in the country was about 15 percent. Today, more than a third of Americans are classified as obese, and rates of type 2 diabetes have doubled since Butz's appointment. Coincidence? Perhaps, but I rather think not, because it just so happens that type 2 diabetes is associated with the consumption of refined carbohydrates, and HFCS is about as refined as carbohydrates get. High fructose corn syrup does not deserve all of the blame for the doubling of afflictions that have killed and sickened millions of Americans over the past few decades (far more, I'll note, than pathogenic bacteria), but it sure as heck deserves a lot of it, a fact that is becoming clearer by the day.

In 2007, for instance, a Rutgers University study found that soft drinks sweetened with HFCS contained "astonishingly high" levels of reactive carbonyls, which are highly reactive (hence their name) compounds associated with unbound fructose and glucose molecules. Reactive carbonyls are not present in table sugar, where the fructose and glucose components remain bound together and are chemically stable. None of this would be a problem if not for the fact that reactive carbonyls are widely believed to contribute to diabetes—particularly diabetes in children.

More recently, a 2010 study by Princeton University demonstrated that male rats given access to water sweetened with HFCS became obese, while those fed water sweetened only with table sugar did not. The Princeton researchers could not say with certainty why HFCS appeared to cause obesity while table sugar did not, but the answer may again lie in the reactive carbonyls, which are more readily absorbed and utilized than the bound fructose and glucose molecules in sugar.

The upshot is that the trend of skyrocketed diabetes and obesity in this country is not expected to level off anytime soon. In fact, the total number of Americans with type 2 diabetes is expected to double in the next 25 years (but then, considering the number has already doubled from where it was a decade ago, we might well beat that by a wide margin). For most of us, that's terrible news, because type 2 diabetes is associated with blindness, kidney failure, heart disease, and stroke, among other things you don't want to deal with. In the boardrooms of the pharmaceutical companies that manufacture the drugs used to treat diabetes, it's a case of turning lemons into lemonade. Really, really sweet lemonade: Already, diabetes drugs add $5 billion annually to the pharmaceutical coffers (never mind the loot they collect from selling the medications used to treat the disease's complications).

And there's this: Thanks to agribusiness subsidies, we're actually paying many times over for the privilege of being fattened and sickened by corn. According to research conducted by the Cato Institute in 1995, every dollar of profits earned by Archer Daniels Midland's corn sweetener operation costs consumers $10 in subsidy payouts.

The good news is that consumers seem to be catching on: Over the past decade, consumption of HFCS has actually declined from its peak of 45.4 pounds per year, a decrease that can almost surely be credited to the rash of studies linking it to disease. The industry response has been nothing if not predictable: In September 2010, the Corn Refiners Association petitioned the FDA for approval to change the sweetener's name to "corn sugar."

14

Despite having interviewed the parents of the stricken child for my *Eating Well* article, I'd yet to actually meet someone who'd suffered a serious case of foodborne illness. This was in part because I didn't want to succumb to what felt to me like the clichéd structure of most food-safety stories, which so often begin with the dramatic and heartrending retelling of an innocent victim who'd been struck down in the prime of his or her life simply by eating the wrong hamburger or piece of lettuce. And it was in part because over the course of researching this book and thinking about the issues at hand, I've become rather intractable in my belief that the presence of pathogenic bacteria simply isn't the most dangerous aspect of our food system.

But it also occurred to me that foodborne illness remains the vector by which most people are introduced to the concept of food safety and that acute illness is still an important piece of the puzzle. To write an entire book about food safety and come no closer to an incident of foodborne illness than a dumpster-diving anticapitalist who puked after he drank fruit juice out of the trash seemed a little specious.

So I found myself dialing Bill Marler's phone number yet again, in hopes that he might provide me with a likely candidate. Now, perhaps I should have expected this, but nonetheless I didn't: Asking Marler to connect me with a victim of foodborne illness was like asking a chef what I should eat for dinner. "What do you want?" Marler asked me. "Hamburger? Spinach? Raw milk? You want a kid or an adult? *E. coli* okay with you?" At first, I thought he was making a joke about the tragic depth and breadth of his clients, and I started to laugh. But Marler was quiet, and I soon realized he was utterly serious.

Which is how I came to find myself knocking on the door of Chris, Holly, and Margot Standish at 9:30 on an exceedingly warm September morning. The door was attached to an attractive red-clapboarded colonial-style house in the town of Glastonbury, Connecticut, located a few miles southeast of Hartford.

Glastonbury is an affluent community of about 32,000. As of 2007, the median household income was over $100,000, and in the summer of 2010, even during the depths of the national real estate malaise, the median sale price of a home was $353,500. The Connecticut River borders the western edge of town, and Main Street is lined with houses that date as far back as the late 1600s, most of them beautifully restored to their historic splendor. It is, in short, a really, really nice place, and in some vague way I can't quite define,

I was surprised that someone from such a pleasant and obviously well-off community could contract a foodborne illness. But of course, that's ridiculous: Bacteria don't discriminate on the basis of socioeconomic status. Or any other status, for that matter.

Chris and Holly Standish are in their forties, well educated and gainfully employed (assistant director of grants and contracts at the University of Hartford and fund-raising consultant to nonprofit agencies, respectively). They moved to Glastonbury in 2005; financially speaking, it was a bit of a stretch for them, but they lucked into a nice house that needed a little work and were able settle into a neighborhood that, on pretty much every front, resembles the epitome of the American dream: affluent, friendly, picturesque, secure. The deeply historic nature of Glastonbury must have been particularly appealing to the Standishes, for Chris is a direct descendent of Myles Standish, who traveled to America on the *Mayflower* and was hired by the Pilgrims to serve as military advisor for Plymouth Colony.

The Standishes have one daughter, Margot. She is 10, and she is the reason I found myself knocking on their door on that September morning. On June 26, 2008, Margot drank a glass of unpasteurized milk purchased at Glastonbury's Whole Foods Market. Like most people who consume raw milk, the Standishes are the sort of food consumers who seek out nutritious food and are willing pay a premium for it. At the time, they believed that raw milk, which they'd consumed for about 6 months, fit perfectly into their food-related ethos.

The milk they were drinking was produced nearby at Town Farm Dairy, a modest enterprise owned by the town of Simsbury and managed by the Friends of Town Farm Dairy, a nonprofit group of local volunteers who had saved the 70-acre farm from financial ruin a half decade prior. The farm's mission was entirely noble: to provide food to the town's neediest residents, educate the local community in matters of small-scale agriculture, and achieve economic viability. They kept a herd of about 35 cows and sold milk directly from the farm and at local retail outlets (Connecticut is one of 10 states that allow raw milk sales at the retail level). Chris and Holly felt good supporting such an enterprise, and they believed in both the health benefits and the safety of the raw milk the dairy provided to its customers.

And so when, on June 28, Margot became ill, they didn't think much of it. After all, her illness began as countless childhood illnesses begin: with diarrhea and intestinal cramping. She was drinking water but not eating, and the Standishes assumed they were dealing with a garden-variety stomach bug. A day or two of bed rest, some dry toast and lots of fluids, and Margot would be back to her precocious self.

But Margot didn't get better, and on the first of July, they called her pediatrician. "There's a bug going around," he told them. "It could last 10 days or so." So they waited through another hellish week, carrying Margot from bed to bathroom and back again, their daughter wailing in agony as intestinal cramps wracked her young body. Finally, on July 8, with no improvement in their daughter's health, Chris and Holly took her to the ER, where a nurse drew Margot's blood. "And that," said Chris, "is when the shit hit the fan."

That's because Margot had hemolytic uremic syndrome (HUS), that potentially deadly complication of *E. coli* O157:H7. Her kidneys had all but stopped functioning, and she was prepped immediately for surgery to insert a PICC (peripherally inserted central catheter), an intravenous line that is threaded through a patient's veins until its tip rests next to the heart, at the cavoatrial junction. When patients need prolonged intravenous therapy, PICC lines are used to reduce the inflammation and pain associated with traditional intravenous access. Margot's chances of survival were pinned at 50 percent; Chris and Holly were told to prepare for the worst.

The worst did not happen, a fact that was made abundantly clear to me as Margot led me on a high-energy, narrated tour of the Standish residence. She is a slight girl with straight blond hair of medium length. She wore glasses, wool-lined slippers, and a shirt that read I ♥ CANDY. In her room, a neat affair despite the presence of dozens of stuffed animals (I was informed that she kept another 100 in the attic and 23 in the basement), she introduced me to Mr. Mouse, a tiny stuffed mouse for which she'd handwritten miniature business cards that could be read—and just barely—only with the aid of a magnifying glass. "Visit my website www.mrmouse.com. Willing to look at things you can't," read one. Another: "$20 off, no expenses paid."

"Twenty dollars off means you only have to pay a penny," Margot explained.

"You mean the regular price is $20.01?" I asked.

"Yes. He's a very particular mouse."

I found Margot to be utterly charming, exceptionally intelligent, and possessing a fine sense of humor. ("I like all animals."

A pause. "Except ones that bite me.") She implored me to eat nasturtium petals (a favorite of hers, and not bad, actually) harvested from the front yard, and she brought me a perfectly ripe cherry tomato grown in the garden by the front door. "Hey, do you want to taste a sweetness?" she asked, her small palm extended to offer the tomato. Her health is by all accounts excellent; she is thin, but not unnaturally so. She is not on dialysis, nor does she take any medications. Considering how close she came to death by HUS, these are minor miracles. It is all but certain that her kidney function has been compromised, but tests will wait until she has gone through puberty, when a more reliable, long-term measure of her kidney health can be applied.

It is true that Margot may yet suffer long-term health consequences from her illness. It may just be that they haven't yet revealed themselves; for instance, pregnancy is hard on the kidneys, and should Margot ever decide to have biological children, she could experience dangerous complications. But that is a concern that may (or may not) be realized many years from now, and for the time being, she is by all accounts and appearances a happy, healthy, and delightfully imaginative 10-year-old.

And so at the time of my visit, the greatest consequence of Margot's illness seemed to be the psychological scars it has wrought on Chris and Holly. Another casualty is Margot's fondness for pudding, a mainstay of her hospital diet. "I used to like pudding, but just so happens that I ate the pudding, I threw up the pudding, and now I don't like it," she told me. Then, to be sure I wasn't getting the wrong impression, she offered this assessment. "When I wasn't throwing up, it was really fun being the hospital."

To be sure, there is no pudding to be found in the Standish residence, and certainly no raw milk, nor raw cheese, even that which meets the FDA mandate of a 60-day aging process. The Standishes don't eat out much anymore, because they feel they can't trust food that's prepared behind closed doors, and they no longer purchase ground beef. Instead, they buy cuts of meat and grind their own, which Chris then cooks with the aid of a high-end meat thermometer that he reluctantly admitted cost $100. Vegetables and fruits are scrubbed relentlessly. "I just assume someone peed on it," Chris told me.

We sat and talked in the sunroom; right outside the screen door, Margot was painting a rock with mushed-up dogwood berries. Bad Company played on the stereo, as it had since I'd arrived an hour prior. Chris, who is tall and thin and keeps his hair just long enough that he could pass for an aging rock star himself, sat across from a sofa where Holly and I were perched. She is of medium height, with neatly trimmed hair going gray. She smiles widely and frequently and possesses a trusting warmth that she has clearly passed on to her daughter.

The changes to their dietary habits seem only logical, particularly given what they now know about foodborne pathogens. More damaging is the nagging sense that perhaps Margot has been affected in ways that may not yet be known. One of the unseen side effects of HUS is that fragments of red blood cells can become lodged in the small vessels of the brain. This was likely the cause of Margot's hallucinations during her 2-week stay in the hospital. "At one point she gave me this piercing look and said, '*It's all a game*,'" Chris told me. He gave a little involuntary shudder. "That's what haunts me

. . . wondering what happened under the surface that we can't attribute." Even after Margot recovered from the initial physical damage of HUS, her performance in school suffered in ways that were difficult to explain, though she has since rebounded.

Not long after Margot became ill, Chris and Holly, with the help of Bill Marler, sued Whole Foods. They were awarded a settlement, one stipulation of which is that they not speak disparagingly of Whole Foods to the press. Immediately upon my arrival, they had me sign a statement that reads, in part, "To any inquiries regarding the fact or settlement of any lawsuit their response will be, 'The parties have agreed that it is in their mutual best interest not to discuss or comment on the dispute in any manner.'"

Although we did not speak specifically about their settlement with Whole Foods, it was clear to me that the Standishes have struggled with their role as claimant. They were careful to explain that Connecticut does not award pain and suffering damages, and that money from the settlement was retained in Margot's name, not theirs. As someone who will likely suffer from diminished kidney function for the remainder of her life, Chris explained, she will need to maintain a generous health insurance policy. The money would help her do that. But they seem keenly aware that not everyone is likely to have empathy for their position. "I know people on the other side of the issue look at us and say, 'Well, you were the damn fools who bought the stuff,'" Holly said. "But it was presented to us as being safe. We're not milking the system." If she was aware that she'd just punned, she made no indication.

Not surprisingly, Chris and Holly Standish have thought an awful lot about how food is produced and distributed in this country. And not surprisingly, this thinking, coupled with their daughter's illness, has made them distrustful of the food system at almost every level. "Clearly, it's not working very well for us to have faith in a system that's not going to protect us," Holly said. I understood that when she said "us," she meant the broader "us," not the "us" that comprises Chris, Holly, and Margot Standish. Because by now, Chris, Holly, and Margot Standish no longer have that faith or the expectation that the system will protect them.

There are varying degrees to their lack of faith: Raw dairy owns a special spot atop the hierarchy of their distrust, but it clearly infuses almost every contact point between them and their food. They have come to believe that most food in this country is produced with profit—not safety, not nutrition—as the primary motivation, and that the lack of transparency into our food system has created an environment that only increases the risk for outbreaks of foodborne illness. Despite their negative experience with a small-scale producer, they believe that localized production is an important component of a safe food system. They are in general pro–food rights, including the right to obtain and consume raw milk, but this position seemed tenuous, as if they were caught between a broader pro-rights ethos and the fact that their only child almost died from drinking unpasteurized milk.

"We have become more educated, and as we've become more educated, we've become more skeptical," said Chris. They are skeptical of the industrial food system, skeptical of the claims made by raw milk proponents, skeptical of the Connecticut Department of Health (which they found to be frustratingly noncommunicative during their ordeal), and skeptical of the public's ability to make sound food choices, particularly given the aforementioned lack of transparency.

When I asked them how, given their experiences and the resultant sense of distrust, they managed to eat anything at all, Chris answered without hesitation. "I guess we're all in denial on some level."

I'd asked if we might visit Town Farm Dairy, which ceased operations shortly after one of its cows tested positive for the same strain of *E. coli* that sickened Margot, about a month after she entered the hospital. We all piled into Chris's Honda and wheeled through downtown Glastonbury, where a "fitness fair" was under way on the small town green. "Hmm . . . ," said Chris. "A fitness fair. Why is everyone sitting down?" I liked his sense of humor, which leaned to cynical but was not overly acidic.

We detoured briefly to the Whole Foods where the fateful milk was purchased and where the Standishes still shop on occasion. The store was busy but not crowded, and the abundance was overwhelming in its color and variety. We breezed past piles of California strawberries and South African grapefruits on a beeline to the dairy case. There was no raw milk to be found; in late March, not long after I visited Mark McAfee, Whole Foods Market permanently discontinued raw milk sales nationwide. Just past the dairy case stood a display of Veggie Booty, the puffed rice and corn snack that was recalled in 2007 following an outbreak of a rare salmonella serotype known as "*Salmonella* Wandsworth." There were 69 reported cases in 23 states. Just past that, a pump bottle of antimicrobial hand soap was situated in the middle of an aisle.

A half hour later, we pulled into the barnyard of the former Town Farm Dairy, now known as the Community Farm of Simsbury. There were no cows to be seen, but a flock of chickens was scratching in the dirt behind a sprawling colonial farmhouse, and through the opening between the house and barn, I could see a few sheep. A group of boys was gathered around a wheelbarrow; one boy hung half in, half out. His playmates were tugging at him, but whether they were trying to push him into the wheelbarrow or haul him out of it, I couldn't tell. A collection of pumpkins was spread across the lawn.

It was the first time the Standishes had visited the farm since Margot's illness. I hadn't known this, or I might not have had the courage to ask. Their unease was palpable. We sat in the car for a minute, as Chris and Holly debated whether or not to park. In the back seat next to me, Margot was engrossed in a book.

"Do you want to get out?" Holly asked.

Chris was quiet for a moment, as he surveyed the scene. "Nah, I don't. I don't want to get out."

He put the car in gear, and we pulled away.

I left the Standishes feeling a little lost. Perhaps this was why I'd originally felt somewhat ambivalent about devoting a chapter to a victim of foodborne illness; after all, what can we really learn from the Standishes' ordeal? That raw milk can make you sick? But I knew that, just as I knew that pasteurized milk could make you sick (remember that the most recent deaths associated with dairy in this country were linked to pasteurized milk), or spinach, or eggs, or hamburger, or pretty much anything at all.

Maybe I'd hoped to make a point about scale. A total of 14 illnesses were linked to the same outbreak that sickened Margot; the source point of the *E. coli* was a single Jersey cow. It's impossible to know exactly how many people might have been sickened by that single cow if the scale of the dairy's operations were larger, but we know that it only takes a few bacteria to make someone sick, and we know how readily *E. coli* can grow and spread. There is little question that the regionalized aspect of the farm kept many people from getting sick. Of course, opponents of raw milk could rightly point out that pasteurization would likely have kept anyone from getting sick.

Or it could be that Margot's illness is a lesson in traceability. Remember, it took the CDC nearly 4 months to determine the source of the salmonella outbreak that sickened 1,800 people last summer. On July 16, 2008, the Connecticut Department of Health notified the state's Department of Agriculture of a possible link between the farm's milk and the outbreak. A week before that, the farm had voluntarily halted retail sales after its own private tests showed elevated coliform bacteria in the milk. This was less than 2 weeks after Margot drank that fateful glass. There is little question that the small-scale, regionalized nature of Town Farm Dairy's operation and customer base enabled a relatively speedy resolution to the outbreak.

Or perhaps the real story is the issue of trust in our food, and how the Standish family has lost so much of theirs, and how if the rest of us only knew what happens out of sight, we too would lose whatever trust remains. The Standishes thought they were doing the right thing, thought that they'd chosen a healthy product, purchased from a retail outlet that would never sell an unsafe food. This wasn't the creation of some faceless multinational corporation. This was a wholesome food produced by well-meaning people and sold through an outlet that has become synonymous with health and vitality. And yet Margot still got sick.

These are all valid points. I suppose any one of them would be reason enough to justify telling Margot's story. But in the end, what mattered most to me were the Standishes themselves and my own recognition, however belated, that the victims of foodborne illness are real and good people, not so different from me and you. This is an absurdly obvious truth, but still it had managed to elude me, in no small part because I'd never spent time with anyone who'd been seriously sickened by a foodborne pathogen. Before I met Margot, the whole notion that one could be made acutely ill from eating contaminated food had seemed somewhat vague and theoretical. Before I met Margot, I'd pretty much dismissed as lawyerly rhetoric Bill Marler's contention that if only our policy makers would take the time and trouble to actually sit down with a victim of foodborne illness, they might be willing to take substantive action. Because meeting Margot and her parents had been affecting in a way I had not anticipated.

But I also recognized a danger, and it is the same danger that I believe has hijacked our national conversation around the subject of food safety. To focus on the relatively small number of people who fall victim to pathogenic bacteria can cause one to lose sight of the larger picture, with all its ongoing and tragic consequences. The hundreds of thousands of Americans who die every year at the hand of diet-related disease can themselves seem like an abstraction, but they are all too real. The overwhelming and overwhelmingly rapid consolidation of our food system into the hands of corporate entities that are intent on turning any final fragments of transparency opaque does not have a sweet face imploring me to sample a nasturtium petal or cherry tomato. The connection between the drug-resistant bacteria that kill tens of thousands of Americans every year and the way our food is produced is real, urgent, and downright perilous; it is also not about to tell you that, except for the throwing up, the hospital was pretty fun.

What I came to understand, as I drove north on my way home from Glastonbury, Connecticut, is that the story of foodborne pathogens and the very real, very charming, and very innocent people who are sickened by them is important not because it presents a comprehensive accounting of the dangers imposed on us by our food. Rather, it is important for exactly the reason I'd been so affected by meeting Margot and her parents: It engages us. It makes it real. It makes us feel. And maybe, just maybe, that feeling is exactly what will compel us to take action.

15

In the waning months of 2010, the battle over food safety and food rights reached a full boil. In late October, FDA officials, accompanied by federal marshals, seized the entire contents of the cheese cave at the Estrella Family Creamery, a 36-cow and 40-goat operation in Montesano, Washington. Twice during the preceding 8 months, portions of the creamery's award-winning cheese had tested positive for listeria, though no one had been sickened.

Following the first positive test, the creamery voluntarily recalled the affected cheeses and conducted a thorough cleaning. Following the second positive test, the FDA requested a recall of all the cheese from the facility, but the Estrella family refused. The listeria, they pointed out, had been found only in the soft cheeses and could only survive in soft cheeses. Why, then, should they have to recall thousands of dollars' worth of hard cheeses, too? The FDA was not amused by the family's lack of cooperation and quickly obtained a court order forcing the seizure of the creamery's entire inventory, valued at about $100,000.

The backlash was instantaneous and seemed centered around two basic points: First, no one had complained that Estrella's cheese had made them sick. Second (and relating to the first), since no one had complained, why was the FDA poking its nose into a small family cheese business? The testing had been conducted as part of a listeria-testing initiative at soft cheese production facilities, many of which were family-scale operations. Was the FDA really concerned about contamination, or was it just looking for an excuse to put the squeeze on artisanal cheese producers, most of which deal in raw milk cheeses?

The food-rights community believed it was the latter, in large part because listeria is an exceptionally common bacterium. "You're dealing with a ubiquitous pathogen," Catherine Donnelly told me. Donnelly is a professor of nutrition and food sciences at the University of Vermont and an internationally renowned expert on listeria. "If you look for it hard enough, you're almost certainly going to find it." This does not make life easy for US cheese makers, who must comply with the FDA's zero-listeria-tolerance policy.

Complicating matters is the fact that there are numerous subtypes of listeria, many of which have not been implicated in human illness. "The FDA is relying on the initial positive test for listeria without doing further testing to determine if the subtype is one that causes illness," Pete Kennedy complained when I called him. Kennedy is an attorney with the Farm-to-Consumer Legal Defense Fund, and he is assisting the Estrellas in their defense. "Even if it is, we don't know if it's present in enough quantities to cause illness."

point is particularly intriguing, given
countries employ a zero-tolerance policy
where small-scale, artisanal cheese makers
on as NASCAR fans at a Kid Rock concert, the
bacter... owledged and allowed, up to 100 organisms
per gram. Are Europeans dropping in the streets from listeria
poisoning? Not according to Cathy Donnelly. "Their rate of incidence is about the same as ours," she told me.

As for the Estrellas, they were living in a sort of cheese-
makers' purgatory. When I spoke with Kelli Estrella in late
November, she sounded enormously tired. Her voice was shaky,
as if she were fighting back tears. The FDA had remained mute
following the seizure; she had no idea what the future of her
family's farm and business held. For the time being, they were
milking the cows (the goats had been dried off for the winter)
and filling their freezer with butter, but this was an untenable
situation over the long haul. "We don't yet know how we're
going to survive it," she told me. "My husband might go back to
logging, and maybe I'll do some cheese-making classes."

But mostly, Kelli Estrella was angered by what she views as
the FDA's trampling of her rights and the rights of the people
who want to purchase her cheese despite the positive test results.
"If someone wants to eat food that's approved by the FDA, they
should have that right. And if someone wants to eat food that's
not approved by the FDA, they should have that right."

As it turned out, I spoke with Kelli Estrella only days
before S 510, the FDA Food Safety Modernization Act, passed
the Senate. The bill was the first major overhaul of the FDA's
food-safety oversight in many decades and, assuming it made

ough the House, would greatly strengthen the agen thority over producers. For the first time ever, the FDA would have recall authority, and food producers would have to write detailed food-safety plans. The bill would also establish stricter standards for imported food and increase inspections of domestic and foreign facilities.

I'd been following S 510's progress for many months, a task that was especially onerous because the bill was living up to an infamous quote by the 19th-century poet John Godfrey Saxe: "Laws, like sausages, cease to inspire respect in proportion as we know how they are made." To S 510 watchers, it seemed as if the bill shifted form on a near-daily basis, as did the perception of its prospects for survival.

Its fortunes were aided by wide-ranging support from numerous consumer advocacy groups, victims of foodborne illness, and progressive food thinkers like Michael Pollan and Eric Schlosser. Attorney Bill Marler was throwing his full weight behind it. Even the corporate food producers seemed to be along for the ride. Everyone seemed to think it was imperfect but less imperfect than most legislation that comes so close to becoming law. An amendment had been attached to the bill; sponsored by Democratic Senators Jon Tester and Kay Hagan, it would exempt producers with less than $500,000 in annual sales if they sell the majority of their food directly to consumers within a 275-mile radius of where it was produced. The amendment seemed to placate many of the local food activists who had previously vilified the bill.

And yet I couldn't muster much excitement. It felt to me as if S 510, with its focus on increasing regulatory oversight and quest for "science-based" risk analysis and production methodology (the term *science-based* appears in the bill 11 times), was the legislative equivalent of not seeing the forest for the trees. The bill was clearly written to address the issue of foodborne pathogens, a consequence that was nothing if not predictable, given the recent spate of outsize outbreaks. But it would do nothing to heal the structural deficiencies in our food system that cause so much long-term pain and suffering.

I was a little surprised to find that Bill Marler agreed with me. Oh sure, he was an enthusiastic, almost rabid supporter of S 510; he'd used his political and industry connections to lobby hard for the bill and had, by his own accounting, spent nearly a decade trying to get something like it passed. "I think the food system is completely fucked," he told me when we talked in early December 2010. By this time, the bill had passed the Senate but was hung up on a legal technicality and was looking as if it might die on the vine. The resistance was "for structural reasons like farm subsidies, cheap food, obesity; S 510 was never intended to address those things," he said. If the bill didn't pass soon, Marler knew, there would be nothing like it for years to come, as the Republican party, which had expressed little enthusiasm for the bill, was about to assume control of the House.

Marler was right, of course. Even if S 510 failed to address the many tens or even hundreds of thousands of deaths included in a more holistic articulation of food safety, what could be wrong with trying to save a few of the 5,000 or so lives that are cut short every year by foodborne illness?

Perhaps nothing, but I couldn't help feeling as if, Tester-Hagan amendment or no, S 510 would only further the trend of consolidation and opaqueness that permeate our food and agriculture industries. Increased regulatory oversight almost never leads to increased transparency. The very existence of the bill seemed to perpetuate the bad bacteria mania that has—quite understandably—gripped US food consumers. Fear was festering, and all of that fear was being directed at "bad" bacteria. It's no secret that when people are scared, they more readily surrender their rights. Although I had not bought into any of the locavore hysteria surrounding S 510—that it would make gardening illegal, for instance—my concern was that it could lead to collateral damage. And that, ironically, such damage would only perpetuate the very problem the legislation was intended to address.

But then, maybe I was crazy. I mean, how could I not agree with Michael Pollan, the current high priest of sensible agriculture and food practices? So I decided to check in with Joel Salatin, the Swoope, Virginia–based farmer who famously introduced Pollan to the joys of chicken processing during the author's research for *The Omnivore's Dilemma*. In the intervening years, Salatin has become something of an agricultural celebrity, in part for his progressive farming methodology and in part for his outspoken views on anything food related. Salatin was in New Zealand when I contacted him by e-mail to get his thoughts on the matter. He was only too happy to weigh in, which is to say, he wasn't happy with the bill at all.

Never before has the government codified, as a food safety issue, its interpretation of production models. Until now, food safety was separate from production practices. In other words, if the tomato came from a compost pile, a fumigated field in California, or a hydroponic greenhouse in Milwaukee, the government didn't care as long as it was free of *E. coli* or whatever.

Now, that will not be the case. The government will codify its science-based production paradigm, and that will jeopardize every alternative production practice out there. Consider what the official government science has encouraged over the years: organophosphates, chemical fertilizer, DDT and other pesticides, mandatory vaccinations, indoor housing for poultry, feeding dead cows to cows, rBGH injections, irradiation, genetically modified organisms, cloning.

The list could go on and on, but the point is that for several decades, official government science has assaulted everything the biological community holds dear. Before now, nobody asked if the chicken was outside or inside. All anybody cared about was that it was pathogen free. With this legislation, production freedom will no longer exist. The test will no longer be measurable contamination but production models that conform to the official government agenda.

In short, Salatin's point was that S 510 or any legislation that addressed the issue of foodborne pathogens was likely to create only a larger divide between consumers and the source of their food. Furthermore, the potential implementation of "science-based" protocols would lead to methodology that would, in almost every way other than pathogenic bacteria, make our food less healthy and ultimately more dangerous.

Still, as 2010 wound down and the new year approached, it was beginning to look as if Salatin and the other opponents of S 510 would be spared. After a brief spurt of momentum, the bill seemed to slide onto the back burner of the legislative agenda. In an e-mail, Marler told me he was "brokenhearted." Still, he did have something to be upbeat about: He'd collected a handful of the moist orbs of manure excreted by his laying hens and sent them out for testing. The results were in, and Marler's chickens harbored neither salmonella nor campylobacter. The chickens were still too young to lay, but when they finally started, Marler could eat with impunity.

Over the course of writing this book, I have been asked many times if my research has made me more fearful of my food or more cautious of how I prepare it. My response to these questions, which typically generates a great deal of surprise, is always "no." In fact, if I were asked to rate my anxiety level as it pertains to food, I'd have to admit that researching and writing this book has made me *less* fearful, not more.

Some of this can be explained by the eating habits my family and I adopted many years ago. We tend voluminous gardens and raise much of our own meat. We are fortunate to live in the center of a small-scale agricultural hotspot, where it's entirely possible to go a full year without purchasing a single food item from a chain grocery store. Our region is lousy with farmers' markets, food cooperatives, and roadside stands, all overflowing with goods that surely were not produced according to "science-based" procedures but that somehow manage to nourish us without making us sick.

But equally, my attitude toward foodborne illness has been shaped by my evolving understanding of bacteria and their role in human life. I now know that, on a physical level, I am not me: I am them. The bacteria residing in my body outnumber my human cells by at least 10 to one. Modern science has woefully little to say about the relationship between our inner ecology and our overall health and even less to say about how the food we eat affects our gut biology. Of course, the approval of the modern scientific community has not always been the best litmus test of what is healthful for us over the long haul. Simply understanding the crucial role bacteria play in supporting human health and life is enough to take the edge off my fear of these microbes.

This does not mean I will never become a victim of foodborne illness. After all, there is only one way to eliminate all of the physical risk associated with food: Stop eating. There'd be no salmonella, no *E. coli,* no listeria, and, because I'd soon be dead, no concern for the long-term threats associated with our food. The truth is this: As long as we choose to eat, we choose to accept a certain degree of risk. We can decide to eat in ways that we believe will minimize that risk, or we can hang out with folks like Edward Gunny. Either way, there is an unknowable degree of risk, and I much prefer that risk to be of my choosing rather than foisted on me by faceless multinational corporations and government agencies. This is my body. I want to feed it and the countless billions of bacteria living within me as I please.

What I have chosen, therefore, is a style of eating that affords me as much transparency as possible. To the extent that I am able, I purchase my family's nourishment from producers operating on a scale or with an ethos that provides a clear view of the where, how, and why of production and processing methods. Admittedly, this is no panacea; the cost associated with this food is often higher than the price of products that come from further up the ladder of consolidation and opaqueness. And as Bill Marler is fond of saying, "Just because you can shake the hand of the guy who sold you your dinner doesn't mean he's not going to poison you."

Indeed. I know that the risk of contracting pathogenic bacteria from my food is small but real. I accept it with every bite I take and with every bite I feed my two young sons, in part because I know that of all the risks associated with the way we eat, this risk is by far the smallest. And I accept it because there is no practical alternative. My food is teeming with bacteria because the world is teeming with bacteria. In this way, food is not so different than me. I find this strangely comforting.

We live in an era marked by a great divide between humankind and the natural biological world. The evidence of the divide can be found at almost every juncture of our relationship to nature, but perhaps no more profoundly than in the way we produce and take our nourishment. The assumption that we can eliminate all potentially harmful bacteria from our food is itself evidence of this divide. This is not to say that we shouldn't utilize commonsense practices to avoid becoming ill, only that attempts to systemically expunge bacteria from our food are certain to fail and likely only to propagate the structural deficiencies that cause the vast majority of suffering associated with the way we eat. Indeed, no one will tell you that S 510 or any legislation can eliminate pathogenic bacteria; no one can say with any confidence to what degree such legislation might reduce the risk. Perversely, such attempts to control bacteria may only exacerbate the danger of pathogenic bacteria by encouraging further consolidation in the food industry.

To anyone who has been affected by acute foodborne illness, the notion that we must accept a certain degree of risk in relation to pathogenic bacteria must sound insane. But we accept risk in many facets of our lives. We strap into seatbelts, submit to TSA (Transportation Security Administration) pat downs, and wear cycling helmets, knowing full well that these measures do not make us immortal. We accept that truth because we understand that life without the risks these measures can reduce *but not eliminate* would be greatly diminished. To eliminate them would require living a life that most of us would find oppressive and, quite simply, not very much fun. We accept the risk because the only way we know to eliminate it is unacceptable.

Already, we live in a time of greatly diminished quality of food and an almost utter lack of food rights. Many of us do not recognize this, because this situation is all we have ever known, but the facts tell the story. If we truly wish to make our food safer, not merely for ourselves but for the generations to come, we will acknowledge and accept the slim risk of pathogenic bacteria. And then turn our attention to the real dangers that affect us all.

As it happens, S510 *did* pass, and on January 4, 2011, President Obama signed the bill into law. This was surprising, but not nearly as surprising as what would soon transpire on David Gumpert's pro–raw milk/food rights blog, completepatient.com, where, it appeared, the ice between Bill Marler and the raw milkers was thawing.

In fact, Marler revealed on January 28 that he'd been in contact with raw milk producers and was interested in helping them evolve their production methodology. *"I spent about an hour today on the phone with one of your frequent commentators (I am sure he would prefer not to mention his name) and I learned a lot about raw milk safety from someone who clearly understands it. I wish him the best and offered to connect him with someone who might be of help in developing a raw milk HACCP,"* Marler wrote.

This provoked the following, from one of Gumpert's frequent commentators: *"Maybe the force is in you after all. Eating pasteurized cheese and wine is like having sex in body condom. Those bubble boy folks smell like latex and rubbing alcohol. Break out and breathe the real air,"* to which Marler replied, *"Now, you have my interest."*

It was all so unexpectedly sweet and chummy that I felt compelled to give Marler a call. "I give them tons of credit," he said, referring to the producers who'd been in touch with him about the possibility of establishing a HACCP plan specific to raw milk production. "They're not just sitting around on a blog, bitching about shit. I think their hearts are in the right place."

I was a little stunned, but not as stunned as I was about to be, as our conversation unfolded into the realm of bacteria and risk. "The problem is, you're dealing with a very complex ecosystem," noted Marler. "Trying to have some rational level of safety in the context of this ecosystem and an industrial food system sometimes just doesn't compute. I wish I had the answer. I wish I had the power to enforce a tax that would force corporate agriculture to get small."

Whoa. Had Marler really undergone a transformation? Were his views on bacteria changing? Was he really thinking of linking arms with the raw milkers to forge a new way forward? He chuckled at my naïveté. "Oh, don't worry. When the next raw milk outbreak happens and I end up representing the families, they'll be calling me a fascist again."

S510 and the Marler/raw milker love fest weren't the only food safety stories of late 2010 and early 2011. Of course, there were still outbreaks happening: carrot juice, sprouts, ground beef, lettuce, and more sprouts. Not a week passed without news of an outbreak or recall. "It's just ridiculous," Marler told me, and I had to agree. It did seem ridiculous.

It was against this backdrop that the CDC quietly released its revised numbers on foodborne illness. There had been widespread speculation that the numbers would be at least somewhat lower, but the drop was precipitous. Rather than the 76 million illnesses, 325,000 hospitalizations, and 5,000 deaths associated with foodborne agents, as had been the previous estimates, the numbers had tumbled to 48 million, 128,000, and 3,000 respectively. Roughly speaking, the CDC had acknowledged that the previous numbers reflected twice as much illness and death due to foodborne agents as actually existed.

Of course, the new numbers were still heavily reliant on extrapolation and assumptions. Indeed, barely 20 percent of the 48 million illnesses were due to known foodborne pathogens;

the rest, said the CDC, were the result of "unspecified agents, which include known agents without enough data to make specific estimates, agents not yet recognized as causing foodborne illness, and agents not yet discovered." Apparently, the agency was accounting for not only the "known unknowns" but the "unknown unknowns" as well.

So, despite the radical revision to the numbers, I couldn't help feeling that the CDC's report was more whimper than bang. It was still an exercise in guesswork. It would likely be amended again in coming years, though whether up or down was anyone's guess. About the only thing I was certain of was that it still didn't tell the whole story of food safety.

16

I was thinking hard about risk and bacteria on a certain evening in late November 2010 as I drove west on Vermont Route 2 to pick up Edward Gunny. Gunny and I had big plans for the evening, which included visits to numerous dumpsters in the central Vermont region and the possible ingestion of foods that would be extremely unlikely to meet with FDA approval.

Nearly a year had passed since my first excursion with Edward, and a few things in his life had changed. For one, he'd moved out of the rented house where I'd been introduced to the unique hell of kettleball exercises and where we'd butchered the deer. Not only had he moved out; he was building a house. This morsel of information threw me a bit, it was hard to imagine someone like Edward ensconced in the domestic bliss of the American homeownership dream. It seemed to contradict everything I knew about him. Land ownership, taxes, a mortgage, home insurance: These did not strike me as Gunnyesque obligations.

Turns out, I needn't have worried, for the "house" that Edward Gunny was building bore a striking resemblance to a garden shed and was perched on a piece of borrowed land. It measured 8 by 12 feet and sat on piers of cemented-together fieldstone. There was no bathroom, no running water. Edward had scavenged as many building materials as possible but was still into it for nearly $4,000, an amount that was tolerable only because he'd gotten a significant raise at his part-time job and was on track to earn nearly 10 grand for the year. "But I'm saving a lot of it," he told me, as if embarrassed to think that I might assume he would spend that much in only 12 short months.

We headed north in my car. (Edward's 1989 Volkswagen had finally given up the ghost a few months prior, and he was carless. In rural Vermont. In the winter.) We were on the very same stretch of highway where, 11 months earlier, we'd spotted so many overturned cars and one road-killed deer. On this night, the weather was much less capricious; it was maybe 30 degrees, and only a dusting of snow lay on the ground. Edward regaled me with stories from his high school years, which included, in no particular order: streaking, expulsion, straight A's, and a dawning awareness that in some very important ways, his future would be different from the future of most of his classmates.

When we reached the city (or what passes for a city in Vermont), Edward and I made a beeline for a historically productive dumpster. He was bullish on the prospects, as this was the same receptacle where he'd procured dozens of pounds of brie the year prior. "It's a good dumpster," he told me. "It's a really good dumpster." This was the first time I'd been introduced to the concept that dumpsters can have merits relative to one another. I must say, it was a refreshing way to look at things.

The good dumpster was located behind a store that sells high-end foods at discount prices. This business model seemed to generate relatively large quantities of discarded products, perhaps because the discount reflected a diminished sense of value, making it that much easier to justify tossing questionable inventory. Or maybe it was because the discount reflected existing imperfections, and the existing imperfections were of the sort that had already pushed the product to the edge of salability, leaving little buffer for further deterioration.

As we pulled up next to the store, I was somewhat alarmed to note that the receptacle sat in full view of a nightclub. Furthermore, on this particular evening, the nightclub was hosting a sold-out show by a pop-punk band known as the Sick Puppies. You're wondering: How big a following could a band called the Sick Puppies possibly have in little Vermont? The answer could be found in the steady stream of ticket holders who walked directly past the dumpster to join the long line that scrolled from the nightclub's front door out onto the sidewalk.

If I expected the presence of a couple hundred onlookers to give pause to Edward Gunny's plans for food reclamation (and to be honest, I did), I was to be sorely disappointed, for in one sinuous, almost athletic motion that held the memory of thousands of such motions over the years, he launched himself into the open maw of the container and disappeared from view. I cast a furtive glace at the bystanders and clambered in after him. We closed the lid over us and flicked on our headlamps.

Dumpsters rarely give up their secrets easily. Oh sure, occasionally you'll have the good fortune to find a wheel of cheese or case of wine perched atop the bags below. More typically, the riches are entombed within the confines of black plastic, where they mingle with nonedible detritus. Liberating them requires pawing through large quantities of garden-variety trash: paper and plastic and packaging. We tend to think of garbage as being sort of gross, but most of it is just cast-off bits of items we handle every day. Sifting through it isn't exactly fun, but from a strictly subjective view of the labor and skill involved, there's nothing particularly challenging about it.

And yet it was clear from observing Edward that truly successful divers have a metaphysical relationship with garbage, a sort of sixth sense for the presence of high-end loot. In the first bag I tore into, I found a box of outdated rice cereal; Edward's first bag contained numerous packages of cheese. I examined one under the glare of my headlamp: $18 per pound. In bag number two, I found dozens of jars of baby food; even among our most countercultural friends, I couldn't think of a single one who would feed dumpstered food to an infant child, so I let the jars tumble to the dumpster's oozy floor. Edward's second bag was home to three unopened packages of chocolate Newman-O's, the organic Oreo cookie knock-off that carries Paul Newman's likeness. We paused for a brief snack.

It took us about 20 minutes to fully exploit the dumpster's potential. Our cardboard box, procured from the recycling container immediately to the left of the dumpster, was overflowing. There were multiple pounds of cheese, perhaps 10 or more. There were the three boxes of Newman-O's (actually, there was a little less, owing to my fondness for cream-filled confections). There was a box of organic crackers. A bag of gingersnaps. A few cans of whole-grain SpaghettiOs knock-offs. We'd found quart containers of soy milk, tempting if only because it would have softened the crumbs stuck to my teeth. But something told me to stay away from it, and I listened. Incongruously, we'd found three pairs of shoes in excellent condition. They were all size 12, which just happened to be the size worn by both Edward and myself. Between the soy milk vibes and the delightful coincidence of the shoe sizes, I was beginning to wonder if perhaps I'd tapped into some of the metaphysical energy that seemed to flow between Gunny and the garbage.

We emerged into a flow of Sick Puppies fans. If anyone was surprised to see two men climbing out of a dumpster, they hid it well. Perhaps such surprise is incompatible with an appreciation of a band named Sick Puppies, or perhaps no one quite knew how to process what they'd seen. Most likely, we were experiencing the strange invisibility of the destitute (or, in our case, the assumed-to-be destitute).

Back at my car, we stood for a few minutes, conducting an inventory of our score, checking the fit of our new footwear, and sampling our wares. Edward was in a reflective mood. "We live in such a strange moment in history," he said, bending to sniff a thick wedge of cheese. "When else would such exquisite food end up in the trash?" He nodded his approval of the cheese and appropriated a slice to the top of a cracker. His mouth opened, and the cracker was inserted. In an instant, the food, swarming with bacteria and accompanied by unknown risk, was gone.

INDEX

269

Enteroinvasive *E. coli* (EIEC),
35–36
Enteropathogenic *E. coli* (EPEC),
35
Enterotoxigenic *E. coli* (ETEC), 35
Enviropig, 201–2
Escherichia coli (*E. coli*). *See also*
E. coli O157:H7
ammonia treatment to kill, 60
in digestive tract, 34
discovery of, 33
enterohemorrhagic (EHEC),
36–37, 44–46
enteroinvasive (EIEC), 35–36
enteropathogenic (EPEC), 35
enterotoxigenic (ETEC), 35
as major food contaminant, 16
milk as vector for, 80
outbreak in 1966, 15
Shiga toxin-producing (STEC),
36, 39
vitamin K produced by, 34
Estrella Family Creamery recall,
249–51
Ethics and morality
GE foods and, 203
profit-based, 68–69, 218
raw milk consumption and, 89
Ethiopia, farmland sales by, 135

F
Farmers
decreasing numbers of, 131–32
difficulties after WWI, 225–26
government seed program for,
142–44
hybridization by, 140–41
percent receiving subsidies, 224
seed saving by, 142
suicide seed technology and,
149–50
Farmland, investment in
disappearance of, 134–35

FBI, Rawsome Foods raid by,
169–70, 183, 215
FDA. *See* Food and Drug
Administration
Fedco Seeds
founding of, 161
Fish. *See also* AquaAdvantage
salmon
author fishing with sons,
189–90
delta smelt, 76
GE salmon, 191–201
Food and Drug Administration
(FDA)
antibiotics approved for
livestock growth by, 112
antibiotics for livestock growth
called "injudicious" by,
122–23
AquaBounty NADA
application, 191
biased voting members, 193–94
difficulties in making rulings,
199–200
Estrella Family Creamery
recall demanded by,
249–51
food rights stance of, 91–92,
186
Food Safety Modernization
Act, 251–56, 259
food safety overseen by, 24
food safety scope of, 27
founding of, 17
frequency of facility
inspections by, 27
GE goats approved by, 192
guidance papers from, 200
misplaced priorities of, 215–19
Monsanto ties to, 28
NADA process defended by, 199
NADA process of approval,
191–202

I

Incubation period of bacteria, 62
Industrial food system. *See also*
    Consolidation
    capitalist model of, 68
    dairies, 81
    disconnect from food due to,
        129–30
    dominance of, 136
    emergence of, 131–34
    faith in, 126
    FDA support for, 92
    food chasing us due to, 133
    increasing scale of, 137
    inescapability of foodborne
        illness with, 67–68
    Marler's critique of, 59, 68
    outbreaks magnified by, 59–61
    power wielded by, 217
    productivity of, 133
    profit-based ethics of, 68–69,
        218
    pushback against, 135–36
    reverence lacking in, 210
    science-based production in,
        252–53, 255
    subsidies supporting, 224
    vertical integration model,
        208–9
Infant mortality rate, global, 33
Irish potato famine, 154

J

Jack-in-the-Box lawsuit, 51–53
Jack-in-the-Box outbreak, 1993,
    23–24, 33, 41, 44

K

Kraft Foods, 131, 134

L

Lateral gene transfer (LGT), 102,
    105, 109, 119–20, 122

Lawn, CR (Fedco founder)
    commune membership of, 160
    on co-ops, 163
    Fedco Seeds founding by, 161
    on seed industry, 163
    upbringing and education of,
        159–60
Listeria monocytogenes
    deaths per year from, 33
    Estrella Family Creamery
        recall, 249–51
    FDA's zero-tolerance policy for,
        250–51
    harmless subtypes of, 250
    as major food contaminant, 16
    milk as vector for, 80
    as ubiquitous pathogen, 250
Locavores, accountability
    achieved by, 67

M

Macrobiotic diet, 176
Marler, Bill (attorney)
    on accountability, 67
    on CAFOs, 61
    career path of, 50–54
    food-safety lobbying by, 53, 55
    on FSIS mission statement, 223
    funnel analogy of, 65–67,
        213–14
    on government intervention,
        69–70
    on industrial food system, 59,
        253
    Jack-in-the-Box case of, 51–53
    on lag between illness spike
        and recall, 212–14
    as leading foodborne-illness
        litigator, 48
    Marler Clark formed by, 54
    motivations of, 52–53
    non-O157 STECS researched
        by, 45–46

INDEX